COMMUNITY COLLEGES

THOMAS E. O'CONNELL has served as president of Massachusetts' Berkshire Community College since its inception in 1960.

COMMUNITY
COLLEGES
A President's View

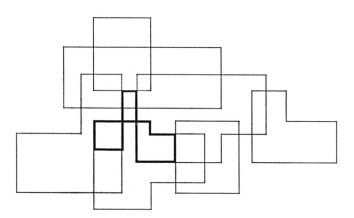

Thomas E. O'Connell

UNIVERSITY OF ILLINOIS PRESS
Urbana   Chicago   London
1968

TO MY FATHER

Acknowledgments

A number of people have helped with this book by making suggestions for it or by criticizing the manuscript. Associates from Berkshire Community College's faculty and staff who have helped include Vice Admiral Robert H. Rice, U.S.N. (Ret.), Assistant to the President; Joseph J. Walsh, Dean of Faculty; F. Brooks Butler, faculty member in English; and Alice Stone Ilchman, former Assistant to the President. Marjorie Rice Fallows, faculty member in Sociology, made a number of useful suggestions. I am indebted to her for a good deal of the material on "low status" students in Chapter 4, and to her and Clara Clairborne Park, faculty member in English, for permission to quote from their articles about Berkshire Community College, as well as to alumna Kathleen Tremblay Evans, Berkshire Community College '62, for permission to quote from her Berkshire Community College Commencement Address of June 1967.

I also wish to thank Irving H. Bartlett, former President of Cape Cod Community College and presently head of the History Department at Carnegie Institute of Technology; William A. Selke, Director of Research for the Peter J. Schweitzer Division of Kimberly Clark Corporation in Lee, Massachusetts; and Robert N. Kreidler, Vice President of the Alfred P. Sloan Foundation. I have used some data assembled by the Director of Planning for the Massachusetts Board of Regional Community Colleges, Donald E. Deyo, and have drawn on conversations with him which reflected his long experience as a community college administrator and former President of the American Association of Junior Colleges. My brother presidents of new Massachusetts community colleges made a number of suggestions for the chapter on how (and how not) to start a community college.

The late Walter M. Taylor, former President of Greenfield Community College, made several very thoughtful suggestions on an early draft of the manuscript just before his death. No one was ever more devoted to the community college idea or gave more of himself to it than Walter Taylor.

The help of my wife and my brother, Jeffrey O'Connell, Professor of Law at the University of Illinois, was most detailed and important of all. I never would have written the book without the spur of my brother and the continuous encouragement of both him and my wife.

Much of the material in Chapter 1 was originally included in two articles written by the author which appeared in the *Dartmouth Alumni Magazine* and *New Republic* in 1964 and 1965.

Responsibility for the opinions and any errors in the book must, of course, be mine alone.

Thomas E. O'Connell
Pittsfield, Massachusetts
1967

Contents

. . . Its heart is in the right place;
its head does not work very well.

Robert Hutchins

1

What in the World
Is a Community College?

In September of 1960 I found myself running an educational bedlam. It was called a community college. It consisted of 150 students of college age and older assembled on the fourth floor of an old, once-deserted, school building in Pittsfield, Massachusetts; three full-time and several part-time faculty members; two secretaries—and me. On the first three floors of the old building were 450 overflow seventh graders from the Pittsfield school system. We had not a single book in our "library," almost no laboratory equipment, and the confidence of only a precious few local townspeople that we could actually make this hastily assembled melange into a genuine "college." *Life* magazine came to cover our college's opening and did a rather devastating job on us. They showed the junior high schoolers swirling around our bewildered college freshmen, our pretty librarian sitting in her library with no books and our equally pretty business teacher in her typing classroom with no typewriters.

1

We were the first state-supported community college in Massachusetts and I was the first full-time professional employee engaged by a new state Board of Regional Community Colleges. I confess that I asked myself as we got those first-semester classes underway, "Can this possibly work?" And even, "How did I get myself into this?"

I had been engaged by the Board largely because of my governmental experience. I had previously been a Deputy Director of the Budget in New York State under Governor Averell Harriman and the Massachusetts Community College Board needed someone to shepherd its budget appropriation to operate the first community college through the executive and legislative branches of the state government. Once that was done, the system would be underway: the establishment of other needed state community colleges would be approved in subsequent years based on the precedent of the first—assuming the first one worked. So when the funds for the first college were finally appropriated, I left the thickets of Boston state house bureaucracy for the Berkshire groves of academe, such as they were, and became the head of the first or "pilot" college.

The idea of community colleges intrigued me, but I had had to overcome some pretty deep-seated prejudices before I decided to be part of one. As a graduate and former administrative officer of an Ivy League college I really wasn't sure in my heart of hearts that quality higher education of the sort I wanted to be associated with could take place outside of a very few elite institutions like the Ivy League colleges, to say nothing of its being developed in a brand new public two-year institution with a very limited budget and with an old school building for its "campus."

It was clear even then, though, that with quality or

without it, community colleges were spreading like wild-fire and were every year educating a larger and larger percentage of each freshman class across the country. Alvin E. Eurich, then of the Fund for the Advancement of Education in the Ford Foundation, was saying that maybe by 2000 there wouldn't be any four-year colleges; maybe there would be only community colleges and universities. I thought it might be fun to be part of something that was moving so fast.

But there were lots of people like me who had no idea what this new kind of college was all about. Since there still are many people who don't understand what we are, let me go back and tell you what a community college is. First, as indicated, it is a junior college—two years. Usually it is coeducational. Usually it is only for com-muting students—no dormitories. It serves a wide variety of students; indeed that is a part of its charm as well as one of its limitations. But there are essentially two groups of students: those who plan to transfer as juniors to four-year institutions and those who plan to take jobs after just two years of college.

It is this multi-purpose quality which accounts in large measure for the community college's surging popularity. Typically a community college has a transfer or liberal arts program containing the same balance among the social sciences, the sciences, and the humanities that one would find in the first two years of a liberal arts college or university. It also has a variety of specialized programs, often called career or occupational or terminal programs. These career programs, in addition to offering a core of compulsory liberal arts courses, include courses to prepare students for jobs in local businesses or industries. In Pittsfield, Massachusetts, the largest employer is the General Electric Company, so Berkshire Community College numbers among its career programs one in electrical technology. Obviously, the more of these career programs the community college can offer, the more opportunity there is for each qualified high school graduate to find the one which suits his particular aptitudes and aspirations. Some colleges have up to twenty of these career programs in fields such as dental technology, nursing, data processing, and the technology of petroleum.

Another reason why community colleges are burgeoning is that they are inexpensive. The first two years of college are cheaper to operate than the last two because larger lecture classes are suitable for many introductory courses (psychology, for example) and because less specialized equipment is required. A nonresidential college costs only about half as much per student to build and run as a dormitory college. The cost to students of attending a community college is a fraction of the cost of a residential college. Many community colleges are tuition free. At Berkshire where the tuition is $200 a year (of a total cost to the college of about $700 per student per year), the *total* college cost to a student living at home is often under $400 a year. This economy makes all the difference to many students from large families or from families of limited income—it often means that they attend college when otherwise they could not even consider doing so.

The community college is also easier to get into. It may even have an "open door" for *any* high school graduate. It is sometimes described as a uniquely American or democratic institution which recognizes the importance of the "average" person's having the opportunity to go beyond high school. The description is justified, I think. The democratic flavor of the community college can be contrasted with what one finds in a technical institute where all the students are in career or occupational programs, or with two-year university branches where all the students are in transfer programs. (University branches, by the by, have the additional disadvantage of being "country cousins" to the main campus. Faculty tend to consider themselves in "Siberia"; they are constantly looking over their shoulders at the main campus.)

At Berkshire we don't quite have an "open door," but we do admit any high school graduate who looks to us like a reasonably good bet to do the job in one program or other at our college. Each year I say to our freshmen, "This is a relatively easy institution to get into, but it is not an easy institution to *stay* in." We have been washing them out pretty quickly when it turns out we guessed wrong at admission—about one-third flunk or quit the first year—but at least they've had the chance, and that's important. And we'll probably have a lower attrition as we initiate more career programs suited to a wider variety of student motivations and aptitudes.

What about the key question that fretted me that first September: the quality of education offered in a community college? The fact that our attrition at Berkshire is high indicates we're not soft. But a community college does have definite handicaps as it strives to keep the right kind of "institutional press" on its students. In the first place, we don't *have* the students for as long as we could wish. They are gone at the close of each day and they are gone after two years. They don't have the benefit of more mature upperclassmen to set a tone for them in the informal, out-of-class education which a residential institution offers. These shortcomings are very real. Cardinal Newman in *The Idea of a University* said that residence with one's fellow students is more important than professors or examinations for "training, molding, enlarging the mind."

The community colleges have other shortcomings. Their students tend to come from the same socio-economic group as well as from the same geographic area, so most of the usual college stimulation of rubbing up against "strange" people is lacking.

David Riesman commented after a study of the University of Massachusetts[1] that the students seemed all very much the same type of person. Most of them are from Massachusetts; all are bright, since admissions standards are higher there than at most state universities because of limited space; most are from families of limited means or they'd be in "prestige" institutions. This homogeneity had a kind of deadening effect on the tone of the University, Riesman thought. Community colleges are apt to be even more homogeneous. Their geographical spread is even smaller, since they are commuting institutions. Students tend to have a narrow, parochial viewpoint; most have traveled very little; most come from families of limited means and limited horizons. Of course, even the selective institutions which strive hard for diversity in their student bodies often end up with a rather homogeneous group of upper middle class students from Palo Alto, California, Shaker Heights, Ohio, and Scarsdale, New York. But that is the fault of their admissions officers and they at least have an *opportunity* to be diverse.

Nor do our community college students get another kind of stimulation often associated with going to college —that of going away from home, of being "on their own." And, of course, two years of college is not really enough of college for most able youngsters, but that is all most of our

[1] David Riesman and Christopher Jencks, "The Viability of the American College," in *The American College*, ed. Nevitt Sanford (New York and London: John Wiley and Sons, 1962), pp. 138–40.

career students get. (Woodrow Wilson is supposed to have said, "Anyone who thinks two years of college is enough has never seen a sophomore. The sap has begun to rise but it has not yet reached the brain.")

Also, the fact that community colleges are less selective in admissions means that there are students in the colleges who are not as well prepared to do what is usually considered to be "college-level" work as would be the case in most four-year institutions. There is a greater disparity in the students' aptitudes and in the amount of information they have than one usually finds in a four-year college. Some students who come to us are very bright, and the community college must not hold them back while attending to the problems of their slower classmates. The problem is akin to that faced by public high schools and we use some of the same devices to solve it. Homogeneous grouping in classes is one device. Many community colleges have several distinctly separate "tracks" for career students, depending on their abilities and the jobs toward which the programs are pointing them. Honors programs, developmental reading programs, special attention to the very quick student and to the slower but especially persevering one are other devices we use to deal with a disparate student body. But obviously the 130 IQ student who comes to Berkshire (and each entering class has several) is going to find fewer intellectually challenging classmates than he would at UCLA or Oberlin.

Cataloging the weaknesses of this new kind of college makes one wonder if Robert Hutchins' criticisms of the community college are not justified. Mr. Hutchins commented: "It is confused, confusing, and contradictory. It has something for everybody. It is generous, ignoble, bold, timid, naive, and optimistic. It is filled with the spirit of universal brotherhood and the sense of American superiority. It has great faith in money. It has great faith in courses. It is antihumanistic and antiintellectual. It is confident that vices can be turned into virtues by making them larger. Its heart is in the right place; its head does not work very well." [2]

As is usual in Mr. Hutchins' acerb criticisms, he is pretty close to the mark. For all the overkill in his statement, it has a core of truth and it is well to have our weaknesses pointed out to us.

On the plus side of community colleges the very least that must be said is: better a community college for two years than no college experience at all. And as a convert after eight years of immersion, I can now assure you that much more than this can be said.

In the first place, community college teachers concentrate on their work in the classrooms and on counseling students. They are not required to "publish or perish." The strongest teachers we can find are given the introductory courses where sparks of interest are most likely to be generated. Since this may in the long run prove to be the most important asset of the community college in making a special place for itself in the pattern of higher education, I reserve Chapter 2 for a discussion of community college faculties.

Many of the community colleges are small. At Berkshire we have about 800 full-time day students in our eighth year of operation, and we won't go above 1,500 for several years. This means we are quickly able to single out for extra attention the really able student or the one with special problems. Our being small means that many students are able to take on leadership functions they might otherwise not have. Extracurricular activities do play a part in commu-

[2] Robert Hutchins, reported in Bert Schwartz, "Is It Really Higher Education?" *Saturday Review*, December 19, 1964, p. 52.

nity college education, though there is relatively more emphasis on the curricular work and perhaps less danger of a marginal student being dazzled by the appeal of a variety of college-subsidized activities to the detriment of his studies.

For many students, attending the first two years of college while living at home is just right. For one reason or another, seventeen is not the right age for everyone to try his wings away from home. I recall the late Dr. Alan Gregg of the Rockefeller Foundation chiding educators for our pride in the slow-maturing nature of humans, and for our paradoxical insistence that full maturity be assumed at the arbitrary cutoff age of seventeen or eighteen. The so-called "late bloomer" often finds the community college the best garden, the place where he has the best chance for growth. At Berkshire we have helped a number of students who left home to go to a residential college, found it a bewildering or overwhelming experience, especially at a large university, and as a result quickly flunked out. They have come to us, done well, and returned more confidently to the university as juniors. Some community college people refer to this as our "salvage function" and that strikes me as an accurate, if inelegant, phrase. In some cases the younger siblings of these "salvaged" students are coming to Berkshire in the first instance, as freshmen.

The lack of juniors and seniors to set a tone—a deficiency in residential junior colleges which has always struck me as very real—is in some measure offset in community colleges by the liberal sprinkling of more mature people in our classrooms. We have a number of housewives, for example, women in their twenties and thirties who come in to take one or two courses during the day while their husbands are at work and their children are in school. They lend a serious and purposeful tone. So do the older married veterans who find us the most feasible college to attend. These mature people, many of whom were caught in the "tender trap" and found themselves with families before they realized what they had missed in education, are almost wistfully grateful for the chance to pick up the lost opportunity. Their zest and energy in taking advantage of it make them a delight for their teachers and catalysts for their classmates.

This perhaps brings us to the "community" nature of the community college. Our colleges are assumed to be the opposite of the "ivory tower" institutions. One of our missions is to serve the community, to be the educational and cultural focal points in our regions: hence the name "community college." We have adult education programs, lecture series, musical programs and plays, short noncredit courses for special groups to upgrade themselves, and a range of other educational activities for which there is a felt need in our communities. While these functions are performed by lots of other colleges and universities, they are perhaps more central to the purposes of the community college. Last year Berkshire served over 1,200 students in the day, evening and summer programs; we held lectures by Norman Rockwell, Max Lerner, and John Ciardi; we served as the "home" for a local light opera company; we ran a series of seminars for businessmen in the area. But with all that we don't feel we are yet having nearly the impact on our community that many community colleges have on theirs.

One of the exciting things about this community college business is that many communities are having colleges established for the first time. Most of these communities are taking the colleges to their hearts as they would no other kind of institution. They sense what a college can mean to them, much as the upper Connecticut River valley communities did when they vied for Eleazar Wheelock's attention as he made plans for starting Dartmouth College two centuries ago. And what has Dartmouth College meant to the upper Connecticut River valley? Visit Dartmouth's Hopkins creative arts center any weekend and you'll see. (We have a complex of three rooms at Berkshire devoted to some aspects of the creative arts; our Fine Arts faculty call it "Son of Hopkins Center"!) So municipalities and states are building spacious new campuses for their community colleges. They are planning to expand them to meet the crush of college applicants during the next few years. That crush is enormous and it is even now upon us. The number of high school graduates in Berkshire County in Massachusetts jumped 40 per cent in just two years between the class finishing in 1963 and the class which finished in June, 1965. Figures for New York and many other states are comparable. As for the role of the community college in handling this avalanche of students, by 1970 three out of four high school graduates in the nation who go on to higher education will enroll in two-year institutions, according to a study by the Prudential Insurance Company.

The situation in Massachusetts is illustrative: the system is growing so fast it takes one's breath away. Our one "quasi-college" of September 1960 has become twelve genuine colleges. Our 150 students have become 10,000 full-time day students and 5,000 part-time students, a total of 15,000 students served in one program or another. Most of our colleges are now planning or building spacious new campuses so that by 1975 we'll be serving some 50,000 full-time day students and another 30,000 part-time students. Other states can cite even more dramatic growth.

We in the community colleges in Massachusetts and elsewhere, though, must do our best to be sure that coping with this *quantity* doesn't preclude *quality* education. One measure of our quality is how well our graduates do in good four-year institutions when they transfer as juniors. As a matter of fact they do very well. But it may be that over the long pull the community college's greatest contribution will come not in this transfer function, but in helping to meet what Walter Lippmann has called the most pressing unfinished business facing our nation: "the gigantic work of adjusting our way of life to the scientific revolution of this age and to the stupendous growth of the population." By providing the communities in Massachusetts and across the nation with flexible educational institutions committed to offering some form of education after high school to everyone willing to prepare for it, the community college may be a decisive factor in our adjustment to this scientific revolution. Soon a high school education will be insufficient as preparation for any but the most menial job. Even now there are not enough menial jobs for those prepared to do no others. At the same time, our society's need for technicians or sub-professionals is greater even than our need for professionally trained people. The career programs of the community colleges may prove the best way to meet this challenge, both by educating young people coming out of high school and by retraining their elders to adjust to automation and new ways of doing the nation's work.

Whether in the "transfer" program or in "career" programs, though, the most important ingredient in the quality of community college education is the teacher. Let us turn now to the critical questions: How good are community college teachers? How good can they be in the future if they take advantage of their unique position in higher education—a position with no pressure to turn away from students in order to concentrate on research?

A community college is a mother; a university is a father.

A Berkshire Community College Faculty Member

2

Berkshire *vs.* Berkeley

Many of our best teachers in community colleges are non-Ph.D.'s, men and women who were blocked or who could see that they would be blocked from promotion in four-year institutions because they wished to concentrate on teaching rather than scholarship. They are pleased to find a college teaching assignment which does not demand that they continue to divide their energies between teaching on the one hand and working at the frontiers of knowledge on the other. The community college is the place for this kind of person—the university is not.

In liberal arts colleges and in most universities there is a natural dichotomy between lower-division (freshman and sophomore) work and upper-division (junior and senior) work. Lower-division work is largely a sampling of introductory courses in a variety of subjects in the sciences, the social sciences, and the humanities. At the upper-division level the student commences to major in a single discipline of his choice. He may also minor in another discipline of his choice. The bulk of his upper-division work will be in these two subjects. In these upper-division courses he plumbs much more deeply into the subject matter of his disciplines than he has been able to do in lower-division courses.

It follows that there is a natural dichotomy between lower- and upper-division *teachers* as to their basic orientation and purpose. The lower-division teacher should be a "spark-starter." He should be student oriented. His students don't need him to be right up to the minute on new developments. What his students *do* need is that he have the time to make himself available frequently to help them puzzle out the mysteries of the subject. They are typically much less independent than they will become as juniors and seniors.

The upper-division teacher is different. His students have different requirements of him. By the time they are majoring in his field, they know some of the basics and are, or ought to be, fascinated by the new developments, the new books and articles that are being written. That is part of the fun of majoring: to feel one is part of something special and exciting and ongoing. This is true whether the student majors in physics or in the classics. It is the responsibility of the upper-division teacher to pass on to the students his own enthusiasm for the satisfactions that go with erudition. He need not be so much a spark-starter as a "fine brown flame" himself. His own research work tends to keep him on top of developments in his field. His students are now ready for working independently. They need less of their faculty members' valuable time.

The dichotomy between the junior or community college on the one hand and the university with its emphasis on upper-division and graduate work on the other hand is therefore a natural one. It is natural for the *student*, since his objectives are different in the first two years from what they will be in his last two years. It is even more natural for the *instructor*, for not only are the objectives different for the introductory course teacher but the academic preparation and orientation ought to be different as well. As a general rule, the community college is simply not the place for the person who is most excited about investigating new theories. The Ph.D. route is by no means a good preparation per se for the person who is going to spend his working days with freshmen and sophomores. The Ph.D. holder may be unhappy working with these younger students and he won't do the job well if he is unhappy with it.

On the other hand, the person who wants very much to teach but who is not fired up by the fun of investigating and writing, is probably not the best person for a university job that involves mostly upper-division and graduate teaching in addition to investigating and writing. He might be much better off stopping at the master's degree level in his discipline, taking some professional courses in the "how" of teaching, and then making a career of teaching in a community college. (Perhaps, to adapt a phrase, community colleges make sense in putting students "two years before the masters." And this means not only teachers with master's but, we would hope, master teachers!)

In the sciences, particularly, there may be a really enormous difference in approach and interest between the researcher and the beginning college student. People working at the frontiers in science at a university may be in a different world entirely from those who must be constantly dealing with the basic body of knowledge to be transmitted to students in introductory courses. A scientist friend of mine cited the researcher who serves as head of a department of metallurgy in an excellent university who doesn't know basic metal facts because he was trained as a physicist and has never had basic metallurgy courses. Thus, there may be in some sciences not just a difference in *emphasis* but a difference in *kind* between the teacher of the introductory college course and the university investigator working at the outer limits of knowledge in the field.

It is interesting to note, by the way, that while the line in higher education is becoming more precise between the lower-division or community college level on the one hand and upper-division and graduate level education on the other hand, the line between high school and college levels is becoming more blurred, especially for the brightest students who have traditionally been those who went to college. The tendency on the part of the best secondary schools to offer more and more courses previously considered "college level," and the concomitant increase in advanced standing placement in several courses for college freshmen, has obscured the difference in course work for the bright student between his high school senior year and his college freshman year. More and more of the ablest students are starting college with very nearly sophomore standing. At the same time, more and more "average" students are taking their first two years at a community college and then transferring to four-year colleges. In California already this year 75 per cent of all freshmen are in community colleges. These developments plus the increasing obviousness of the natural break in student and faculty purposes between the lower and upper divisions is making more definite the distinction between the first two years of college and the last two.

To extend the analogy upward, there are, of course, definite distinctions between the four-year undergraduate institutions and university graduate schools. The principal differences that obtain between lower and upper divisions in undergraduate education also exist between upper-division undergraduate education and graduate education: the students' purposes are different, the faculty's purposes are different, and the higher level of study is much more expensive. It is becoming apparent, though, that there may be *less* basic difference between upper-division undergraduate education and graduate education than there is between upper- and lower-division education at the undergraduate level. That is why the experiments in new universities in Florida and in Staten Island in New York City are so interesting. Those institutions will be exclusively for juniors and seniors and graduate students. Their students will all be community college transfers. Perhaps this will prove to be a more viable division of labor in the higher education pattern of the future: there will be two-year colleges for freshmen and sophomores and universities for juniors, seniors, and graduate students, as Alvin Eurich predicted.

To return to the preparation of teachers at the various levels, what happens to the typical Ph.D. aspirant, unfortunately, is that he does lower-division teaching as a young graduate student at the university, when he is least prepared to do it. The great universities, it is generally acknowledged, especially by students who have attended them, are strongest in their teaching as the student goes up the academic ladder. Introductory courses, taught by young graduate students, sometimes in large sections, are apt to be less than exciting. The graduate student may have little interest in teaching and even less interest in students only slightly younger than himself. (Isn't it a phenomenon of growing up that we tend to view the age group immediately younger than our own as a pretty sorry lot?) Only when the student begins to major in the department of his choice is he apt to get the "name" faculty people who made the university glitter for him when he applied for admission. And he may not have many exposures to them until he begins graduate work.

Thus, a Berkshire Community College is strongest where a Berkeley is weakest. At Berkshire Community College we make it our special business to attend to the needs of all of our lower-division students. The central problem at the University of California at Berkeley has been that attending to the needs of the students—especially young students in introductory courses—has been an ancillary responsibility of a high-powered and brilliant faculty for whom investigation is incomparably more important and rewarding. The students sensed this and rebelled.

A young faculty member from Berkshire Community College moved to the Berkeley campus just before the student riots there. She reported on the contrast between the attention given to the freshman at Berkshire and that which the Berkeley freshman could get. Faculty members in one social science department at Berkeley had for a time refused to put their names on their office doors, using the excuse that all members were available for an hour once each week through an institution known as "the bull pen"—one hour a week for consultation with all their students.

She reported that even the genuine concern of a teacher at Berkeley who gives a whole afternoon to seeing students cannot go very far in a class of several hundred when many students wish this contact. The waits can be long, often in corridors without chairs and inhospitable to lingering. The ultimate interview can be full of strain as the student confronts a weary professor and at the same time remembers the line of students still sitting outside on the corridor floor. It may take brashness and persistence to see some faculty members. Our former Berkshire Community College faculty member herself was employed at a research institute on area studies, one of many such specialized research organizations ringing the Berkeley campus. She reported that these were the places where some Berkeley faculty members could *really* get away from their students, where they could be certain of absolutely no student interruptions in their scholarly pursuits. Other Berkeley faculty members avoid student interruptions by simply staying at home to write (as I am doing as I work on this book!).

Now, of course, productive scholars *must* have uninterrupted time. But the point is that it is difficult for the scholar to *divide* his time and his purpose between investigating and being available to his students. This is especially hard for him to do if he has large numbers of students in his classes, as is the case with many teachers of introductory courses, and if the students he will be seeing are just learning the first steps in his discipline and are therefore not the kinds of people he can get much stimulation from with respect to his own scholarly pursuits.

The decision as to how he will spend his time can become a very personal and very much a day-to-day thing for the teacher-scholar. I have a brother who is a teacher-scholar at the University of Illinois. He is constantly faced with the tough decision: how shall I spend, say, the half day immediately ahead now that my classes for today have been taught? Shall I stay in my office where I know I'll be interrupted by students or shall I hole away in the library, where no one can find me, and slug away at my book? He usually opts for the latter course because there he has tangible deadlines and there is where he will make his reputation in his field. He likes students. He is popular with them. Good education would take place in his office over a cup of coffee with students. But the pressure on him is greater the other way. He does not happen to teach freshmen or sophomores, but the pressures on him to decide daily between students and scholarship are not significantly different for his colleagues who *do* teach freshmen and sophomores. And it is these younger students who are, to repeat, less independent and *need* more attention than upperclass students and graduate students.

The pressure to publish at a large university like Illinois or Berkeley is only one of the forces which divert the time of the faculty member from his students. Another might be called "professionalization." This equally intense pressure dictates to younger faculty members how their time and energies should be allotted. It comes chiefly from senior departmental members on whose good offices ultimately depend hopes for promotion. Student advising, extracurricular events with students such as debates, panel discussions, special seminars, redefining undergraduate major requirements, interdisciplinary courses are all nonprofessional. While not bad in themselves, they dilute the effort of the teacher-scholar toward maximizing his publications and exposure to his peers. Many young enthusiastic teachers can take part and promote student-oriented events only at the risk of displeasing some senior colleagues.

It should be pointed out here that many of the large universities like Berkeley have recently been trying very hard to pay more attention to their students. Our former Berkshire teacher reported that one result of the rebellion at Berkeley was that "some of the faculty finally discovered that we have students on this campus." There are now more faculty members who keep an open door, literally, and who seem to be in dialogue with many of their students—challenging, arguing, and encouraging. (This is mostly, however, with the brightest undergraduates or the graduate students.) The faculty of the University of Illinois at Urbana recently devoted an entire faculty meeting to debating the question: "Is the person devoted exclusively to teaching to be encouraged by this university?" Out of the meeting came the following resolution: "It is the sense of this open meeting of the University of Illinois faculty on the Urbana-Champaign campus that we and the Administration should endeavor to place more emphasis upon, and provide more rewards for, higher quality teaching. To this end we believe it would be helpful for the Senate Committee on Educational Policy to make a study and recommendations with respect to such factors as: (1) Ways of stressing teaching quality and quantity as important elements in salary, promotion and tenure; (2) Ways of developing citations at the Department or College level for outstanding teachers."

There are further signs of progress at the big universities in the growing concern for creating a more intimate atmosphere for their students. Living-learning dormitories where courses are taught right in the living quarters are becoming popular. At the University of Massachusetts about fifty courses are now being offered in dorms-with-classrooms. The device of splitting 2,000 entering students into groups of thirty which stay together for all their freshman classes is being tried at Florida State University at Tallahassee. Cluster colleges are another idea. Certain university facilities are centralized and used by all students —facilities such as admissions and administrative offices, health services, dining, library, and athletic facilities. Around this core of facilities are clustered dormitory colleges operating as semi-autonomous institutions. These ideas, while full of potential, usually face opposition by faculty who may find them threatening and by holders of purse strings who find them expensive experiments indeed. They are, though, encouraging efforts to do in the university situation what we in the community colleges put our primary emphasis on: that is, to attend to the needs of the students.

At our community college our Dean of Faculty tries to relieve the faculty member of the conflict as to what he should do with his time. It is made clear to the faculty member that the students are his main concern. The Dean expects the faculty members to be available to students. If that is not what they want to do, they shouldn't be in a community college. Usually it is *just* what they want. Many of them are former university teachers who found my brother's dilemma in choosing between students and writing to be an intolerable one, especially if their own daily preference had been to spend time with students despite their realization that the Ph.D. *must* be completed, or that publication *must* be forthcoming. One of the problems with staying in the university setting for them was that their scholarship would probably have been less than first rate and they knew it. How much of the worthless, dry-as-dust, jargon-filled nonsense produced in our scholarly journals these days is the result of teacher-scholars producing articles because they feel they simply must produce?

Many of these teacher-scholars ought to be *teachers*. They are in education because they like students and like to teach. They like working at the level of higher education. They don't necessarily write well and their curiosity and originality and investigating abilities are less than a really useful scholar needs. Why shouldn't they simply teach, especially when they are able to demonstrate that they can teach freshmen and sophomores well and are happy to do so?

All this is not to derogate the university teacher-scholar. On the contrary, the point is that the person who can teach well and also investigate with distinction is a rarer bird. He is harder to find and his teaching should be in more advanced courses where his research is more apt to complement his class work. The good teacher who is *not* a good investigator is a much less rare type and he should teach the more numerous freshmen and sophomores. He should be spared having to go through the charade of producing original scholarly work—which he can make original only through triviality or petty controversy which no one reads or pays any serious attention to anyway.

To summarize, since more and more first-year students will be entering community colleges in the future simply because of the pressure of numbers, it is natural that the noninvestigator college teacher should be hired by the community college to concentrate on what he does best and what he likes to do—teach and deal with students. He will prepare the students better for upper-division work than can the graduate student who is a part-time teacher at the large university.

There are two key problems in this argument for acknowledging a definite difference between the university teacher-scholar and the lower-division or community college teacher. One is: how do you find and educate the latter in graduate schools where all the pressures on the graduate student are to prepare to go on to the doctorate? The Master of Arts in Teaching programs designed to prepare secondary school teachers have stubbed their toes on this obstacle. So deeply ingrained in our graduate schools is the idea that stopping short of the Ph.D. is to settle for something less than the best, even for the graduate student who is obviously not research oriented, that it will take a revolution to change the philosophy of graduate education, especially graduate education for college teachers. Of course, the revolution is upon us: the numbers of college teachers who must be prepared in the next few decades to handle the flood of college-bound high school graduates will ride roughshod over resistance to the concept that master's degrees ought to be the standard preparation for a college teacher—especially a lower-division or community college teacher. Most university presidents feel that a decade from now there won't be nearly enough Ph.D.'s to go around even for their upper-division and graduate level teacher-scholars, particularly with the demand for Ph.D.'s on the part of business and government. (I should point out that not all university presidents see it this way: New York University Chancellor Allan M. Carter, for example, flatly disagrees.)

Maybe it will be a healthy thing for graduate schools to be forced by the numbers problem to abandon the idea that every college teacher must be a working scholar and must have a doctorate to demonstrate it. Maybe it will also be a good thing for the numbers problem to end the silly war which has been waged for too long between professional educationists in our graduate schools of education and the scholars in our discipline-oriented graduate and professional schools. What a paradox it is to have future college and university teachers coming up through our graduate schools without being required to take a single course in the methodology of teaching and then having to work out classroom techniques for themselves by trial and error! That paradox is almost as sorry an indictment of our standard graduate and professional schools as any of the revelations of Conant[1] or Koerner[2] regarding the graduate schools of education.

We need to have (and therefore will eventually get, I believe) flexible graduate education designed to prepare a lower-division or community college teacher. It can't be composed only of courses like those which have for years been preparing primary and secondary teachers, that is, the educationist's certificate requirement program stressing methodology to the point where it drives out the liveliest students. And it shouldn't be composed only of study in great depth of one aspect of the discipline as has been the case of Ph.D. programs in the past. It must be something new. The emphasis must be on the discipline itself, but there must be a few professional education courses as well—courses in educational psychology, tests and measurements, and audio-visual aids, for example. And graduate work to the level of the master's degree should be sufficient.

Roger Garrison of the American Association of Junior Colleges describes in a thoughtful report on junior college faculty problems[3] how such a sixteen-month or two-year master's program might work. It would include a minimum of ten courses in the subject discipline at the graduate level. Some of these courses should, if possible, be interdisciplinary in content and in instruction, such as geography-geology-ecology or literature-art-music. While courses are being taken, there should be one quarter or one semester of part-time teaching done at a com-

[1] James Bryant Conant, *The Education of American Teachers* (New York: McGraw-Hill Book Co., 1963).
[2] James D. Koerner, *The Miseducation of American Teachers* (Boston: Houghton Mifflin Co., 1963).
[3] Roger H. Garrison, *Junior College Faculty: Issues and Problems*, American Association of Junior Colleges (Washington, D.C., 1967), pp. 70–74.

munity college close by, with supervision by a veteran teacher at that two-year college. There should be a professional seminar involving all students in this master's program (not just those of one department). The seminar might meet for a couple of hours every other week through the entire period of the graduate program and replace, in effect, specific professional courses such as educational philosophy and teaching methodology. The seminar would be led by teams of graduate professors and senior faculty members from nearby community colleges. Garrison's proposal is the result of conversations he had with community college faculty members throughout the country on what they thought the graduate education of future colleagues should consist of. So it reflects the ideas of people who are themselves teachers of introductory courses rather than university teacher-scholars.

After all, most people are attracted to academic life by a passion for their discipline and by an interest in teaching and in students. Only secondarily do a fraction of those people subsequently become intrigued with writing or with making breakthroughs in knowledge. The present system of graduate education refuses to recognize this order of interest and the system must be revised.

It is particularly important that this new graduate education be flexible so that it will permit mature people in other pursuits who have not previously thought of teaching as their occupational goal to turn around in their career plans and teach at the college level after several years of doing something else. We are going to need so many new people in lower-division and community college teaching that we must tap this resource as well as the more conventional one of twenty-three- or twenty-four-year-olds coming out of the graduate programs. A vice-president of the General Electric Company who was the top ranking man in the large Pittsfield General Electric operation recently resigned his post to join our faculty at Berkshire Community College. He had previously had some academic experience and had done some part-time teaching. But what if he hadn't? Shouldn't there have been a route for him to enter academe? College teaching has great appeal for able people. We in higher education must make it easy for people in their thirties and older to shift gears and come to us. They can't typically take the time to get Ph.D. degrees and they needn't be encouraged to do so. But they ought to be able to get degrees in, say, a Master of Arts in Community College Teaching.

In Massachusetts and in other states, community colleges have been working with the state universities to establish master's programs similar to those described by Garrison or to the more familiar M.A.T. programs for secondary-level teachers. Gradually these programs are producing a few lower-division and community college teachers. Unfortunately, Ph.D.-oriented graduate departments look somewhat askance at them and thus the more promising graduate student is wooed into the doctoral programs by informal pressures if not by fellowship money which the department chairman dispenses. Thus, in turn, the graduate student pointing at community college teaching is apt to be last in line for fellowship assistance behind the department's doctoral aspirants.

In spite of this "guild" resistance, these master's programs are receiving some support and my guess is they will receive more as the need for them becomes clearer. Perhaps liberal arts colleges can help. Peter Muirhead, Associate Commissioner of the United States Office of Education, has suggested that with federal help liberal arts colleges might enter into cooperative arrangements

with community college systems for the preparation of
of two-year college teachers. These master's programs
might be one answer to the enormous pressure the liberal
arts colleges are under to enter into more graduate programs. Since these programs would be discipline-oriented
and not Ph.D. level, perhaps the liberal arts colleges could
undertake them without losing their distinctive, under-
graduate-oriented flavor. Through these programs they
might move into graduate education without apeing the
big universities, which many thoughtful liberal arts college
presidents are very reluctant to do.

I don't know, but I'm prepared to bet that community
colleges would benefit a great deal more from concentrat-
ing jointly with other institutions on programs to prepare
teachers than we will from current efforts to prepare community college administrators. There are a number of
centers established at universities around the country,
generously financed by the Kellogg Foundation, called
Community College Leadership Programs. My hunch
is there will be too much "slippage" from these programs
for them to get us many community college administrators who will still be in community college work ten or
twenty years from now. They'll end up doing something
other than the program is specifically pointing them at,
as my public administration graduate school classmates
have done. I'd rather see us prepare *teachers:* some of
the teachers would become administrators inevitably, and
probably they'd be better than those who go into a leadership program specifically to become a dean or president.

At this point, I ought to admit that good, and certainly
great, teaching is not achieved simply by giving faculty
members who are interested in teaching plenty of time to
concentrate on teaching. Good teaching—and certainly
great teaching—is a subtle and mysterious thing. Too

often it does not equate with anything. Those who say that only people on the frontier doing research are good teachers are wrong and those who say people on the frontier doing research are bad teachers are wrong. Those who say that people with time to teach who love to teach are necessarily good teachers are also wrong. There *is* no pat formula. Hurried, harried people can be great teachers; leisurely avuncular souls can be terrible. Gregarious people—socially exciting—can be awful teachers; mousey, shy —even inarticulate—types can be great ones.

To admit, though, that the capacity to be a good or even great teacher is a very elusive business does not mean that we should throw up our hands and do nothing to organize our higher education system to foster good teaching. On the contrary, it means we must do all the more to construct things *around* that elusive quality so that the structure makes as much sense as possible. Granting the mysterious quality of good teaching and granting that it can flower or wilt under almost any system of higher education for reasons no one completely understands, I would maintain that it still makes sense to separate in a measure the citadels of research and advanced work from the citadels of teaching and beginning college work. It also makes sense to create an honored and acknowledged place for those who want to teach and counsel students as contrasted with investigating and publishing. Such an arrangement cannot guarantee great or even good teaching any place, but at least it seems one sensible way to try to get good teaching and happier students, as well as better research in places devoted to it.

There is a second key problem in making this definite distinction between the upper-division and graduate level teacher-scholar and the lower-division or community college teacher-counselor: how is the noninvestigator teacher going to keep up with the developments in his field? I have argued that he need not be as up to the minute as the teacher-scholar who needs to be really *au courant* just to stay ahead of his bright majors and graduate students. Clearly, however, the lower-division or community college teacher cannot completely ignore new discoveries in the substance of his subject or in new ways of teaching the subject. Introductory biology should not be taught today as it was ten years ago. The accelerating rate of change in nearly all disciplines makes it imperative that the lower-division or community college teacher "keep up" if he is to do justice to his students.

I would argue, though, that he can keep up in his field and grow professionally without being a productive scholar himself. The burden for giving him opportunities to keep up with the developments in his field lies with the administrators and board of trustees of his college. It should be made easy for him to attend discipline-oriented summer institutes and short courses on university campuses. He needs sabbatical leaves just as much as his university counterpart. He should have generous allowances for purchasing books and periodicals and for attending professional meetings with colleagues in his discipline. He should be expected to take advantage of these opportunities by his department chairman, one of whose principal responsibilities should be to guard against his department colleagues' becoming complacent and ceasing to keep up. Within the departments themselves there should be meetings devoted to new developments, perhaps with outside speakers invited—scholars from nearby universities, for example.

Some scholars, indeed, believe that it is easier to keep up when one is *not* writing. The person pressing on to finish a book and perhaps get out some articles at the same time may have less time to read generally in his field than a colleague who is not writing. The point usually made about scholarship and its complementary function with teaching is that it keeps one current in a way that bears on classroom presentations. But often it keeps the scholar current only in the narrow area related to his present writing. And his present writing may be so abstruse that it has almost no relevance for an introductory course he may be teaching. His research may make him too interested in the subtleties, the latest wrinkles, which beginning students don't need or can't understand.

In spite of the argument I am making for a distinction to be made generally between the lower-division teacher and the upper-division or graduate teacher-scholar, I hasten to point out that it is healthy for there to be *some* scholarly research being pursued by the lower-division or community college teachers just as it is healthy for us to have a few Ph.D.'s on our faculties, particularly in leadership positions. The basic job of the faculty is teaching and working with students, but this should not preclude research by those faculty members who wish to pursue it. It need not be a primary or continuing responsibility for any given faculty member, but for each department to have some research going on should obviously not be discouraged.

It seems to me that the primary emphasis of all these faculty efforts to keep up—sabbatical leaves, summer institutes, short courses on university campuses, on-campus research and meetings with colleagues from other colleges and universities—the emphasis of all these efforts might best be placed on *how to teach the subject better*. The community college should be looked upon as a laboratory for research in teaching. Our faculties should turn us into innovating institutions for experimentation on curriculums and we should be trying new ways of evaluating teaching. In this sense, the community college itself is on the frontier of knowledge.

The most exciting developments in secondary education over the past fifteen or so years have resulted from concerted efforts on the part of leading secondary school teachers, cooperating with college and university researchers, to devise new ways to get knowledge and understanding across to young people in their early and middle teens. The results of these efforts have been especially dramatic in the sciences and mathematics. Four efforts might be cited: The University of Illinois Committee on School Mathematics (UICSM), established in 1951; the Physical Science Study Committee (PSSC), established in 1956 and centered at MIT; the Biological Sciences Curriculum Study (BSCS), established in 1959 and headquartered at the University of Colorado; and the Chemical Education Material Study (Chem Study), established in 1960 and headed by Nobel Laureate Glenn T. Seaborg and centered at Harvey Mudd College and the University of California. These and related studies, financed largely by foundations, have revolutionized secondary teaching in the sciences and mathematics and thus, of course, have benefited introductory college teaching, too. The example they have set might be followed on a systematic basis by community college faculty members. Three tasks could be undertaken: (1) the original study of better ways to teach introductory college courses, (2) the important follow-up work to test how well the new approaches work, and (3) the process of familiarization with the new approaches on the part of new community college teachers and established teachers to whom the new approaches are unfamiliar. Thus nearly all community college teachers could be involved in the process at one point or another. Of course, sciences are not the only disciplines that can benefit from a thoroughgoing and continuing review as to how best to teach them. Since community colleges are teaching places, perhaps their faculties should become the "tip of the arrow" for improving college teaching just as secondary-level science teachers have been for secondary teaching.

"How do they keep up?" is the most critical question to be asked about lower-division or community college teachers as they become more numerous and more important as a discrete class or category of teachers. It is even more critical, I think, than the important question, "Where do you find them?" Boards of trustees and community college administrators should be judged in the future on the precise and realistic answers they can give to those two questions.

Praise youth for pulling things apart
Toppling the idols, breaking leases;
Then from the upset apple-cart
Praise oldsters picking up the pieces.
Praise Wisdom, hard to be a friend to,
And folly one can condescend to.

In Praise of Diversity
Phyllis McGinley

3

The Multi-Purpose College

The community college is changing the definition of the word "college." It is also making obsolete the concept of considering young people to be of "college material" or "not college material." The word "college" is now something much broader, much more inclusive. Up to recently it has been a word used, especially in the eastern part of the United States, to describe a four-year liberal arts institution which prepared people for a bachelor's degree. It has had an elite flavor about it, a place for the "ins," a passkey to a special world for the elect who could attend. It has not been for those who were "not college material," a wonderfully vague phrase used, I suppose, to describe those whose IQ's when measured imprecisely back in the eighth or ninth grade had been below 110 or so.

We Americans have prided ourselves on not closing educational doors to our children at age eleven, as is done

34

in England. In fact, we have simply closed the door at age eighteen instead. We have labeled as "not college material" the eighteen-year-old who has not yet shown sufficient maturity to belie the IQ test which much earlier cut him off from the elite.

I am always struck by the tone which is used by people (including high school guidance counselors!) when they tell me that a certain youngster who may measure as "average" or thereabouts on one test or another therefore is "not really college material." No one who has worked in a community college could use that expression or that deprecating tone. For we see taking place each year metamorphoses in students which render absurd the placing of people into facile categories or using that hopeless tone. A particular student may predictably never make it to the Ph.D. degree (though I have become leery of making any flat predictions about what a particular eighteen-year-old cannot do), but he may very well be able to cope with a two-year career program. And if he is indeed average —whatever that means—he may very well take fire in the community college and continue on to the bachelor's degree.

Yet some high schools in our area whose graduates we have served for eight years continue to divide their students according to "college preparatory" and "noncollege preparatory" on just about the same basis (basically, eighth-grade performance) and at the same time (entrance to the ninth grade) as they did before Berkshire Community College was established. We then accept some of their "noncollege prep" students four years later anyway (over the automatic negative recommendations of these high schools) and by overcoming great odds some of these students succeed with us. They have been penalized, though, in their high school course preparation by the unwillingness of their elders to change with the times. Our situation is not unique. It is hard for people, and high school guidance officers are no exception, to accept a changing definition of "college" as including something other than a place where one gets a bachelor's degree. Thus, career programs in two-year colleges leading to associate degrees are the ideal answer for thousands of youngsters who are being steered away from them by parents and high school guidance officers who persuade them either to aspire higher than they should—to the revered bachelor's degree—or not to aspire at all. This is true not just in Massachusetts where our associate-degree career programs are new, but even in California where public community colleges first really took hold. Patterns of education change slowly. But the pattern of this change in higher education is coming quickly and dramatically and only gradually are parents and high school guidance counselors coming to realize it.

While high school guidance officers may thus have been measuring their students by obsolete and rigid standards, university and four-year college people have their own conventional wisdom which includes decrying the watering down of "standards" in higher education which results from permitting too many people to go to "college." I always wonder what standards they are talking about. Is there one set of standards in American higher education now? Was there fifty years ago? Or a century ago? Anyone who reads about the history of American higher education in Frederick Rudolph's *The American College and University—A History*[1] must be struck by how *changeable* the academic standards have been over the years, and how *low* they have usually been compared to

[1] Frederick Rudolph, *The American College and University—A History* (New York: Alfred A. Knopf, Inc., 1962).

our present standards. My own guess would be, based on Rudolph's descriptions, that the academic standards at Mark Hopkins' Williams College or Eliphalet Nott's Union College of a century ago were not nearly as high as those of Berkshire Community College today. After all, the main objective of those institutions at that time, as Rudolph points out, was piety and not intellect.

Is there not a different set of academic standards at Williams College today than at, say, the University of Arizona? or Park College in Missouri? or North Adams State College nearby in Massachusetts? Is it *bad* to have differing standards? Is it bad to have a community college like Berkshire which is flexible enough and has had a student body heterogeneous enough to have students succeed very well as transfer students at each of these four-year institutions (as has indeed been the case)?

Four-year college and university people often talk, too, about the fact that many students are going to college who "can't benefit from it." I'm never sure what *that* means, either. (My guess is it means that they don't want to teach any except the brightest students. "Do you have to take many dumb students?" one university person asked me. "We have a lot of average students," was my response.) It ignores the needs of our times to say that everyone should not pursue education as far as he wants to go and *can* go without flunking out. And how anyone engaged in the daily work of education in this country in this time of exploding knowledge can say that any student can get too much education is beyond me. I have never known any American who has "too much education," and I don't know any American who thinks he has too much education.[2] The idea of "too much education"

[2] I confine my discussion to the United States simply because there is some evidence that in India, for example, there are more highly

for anyone in the United States is as silly as the dated definitions of "college" and "college material" which community colleges are helping to revise.

A term that is often used to describe the kind of flexible college I am discussing is "comprehensive community college." It is much like the comprehensive high school in its multi-purpose nature. There are three main kinds of programs: the transfer, career, and adult programs.

Transfer programs in community colleges are set up specifically to educate freshmen and sophomores who plan to move on to four-year colleges or universities as bachelor's degree candidates when they have completed their first two years and have received the associate degree. For them, the associate degree is halfway to the bachelor's degree. These transfer programs are relatively easy to establish, and to understand, because they involve about the same kinds of courses the universities require of their lower-division students. They provide the broad base on which bachelor candidates build their major and minor subject work. A typical transfer program has about one third of the courses in each of the major divisions: social science, science, and humanities. They are, in short, conventional freshman and sophomore liberal arts programs.

Since the bachelor's degree has for decades in this country been the important degree—the "college" degree, the cutting edge between the "educated class" and the rest of the people—many more students come to the community college aspiring to the transfer program than are actually able to handle the rigorous academic work it

educated people than jobs to challenge them at this stage of India's development. In Latin American countries where I have lived there are too many highly educated people in certain professions, particularly the law, relative to the work to be done. But those are special situations.

requires. One of the principal educational jobs which community colleges must do is to persuade high school graduates (and their parents and high school guidance officers) that there are avenues open to them other than those leading to the B.A. or B.S. degree. But for those students who *are* academically qualified and who want and can afford four years of college, the community college transfer programs provide the first half very well.

Let us look at the record. At Berkshire there has been almost no trouble in transferring credits to four-year institutions. As to the work our students do once they get to the four-year institutions, we were pleased (no, overjoyed!) to find that our first group of 111 graduates who went on to forty different four-year institutions with credit for their community college work achieved on an average a 2.45 cumulative index (4.0 equals straight "A") their first semester. We calculate that this would be slightly better than their junior year classmates. Their successors have done nearly as well, despite the fact that we have lately recommended more "risk" students to the four-year institutions since our first transfers did so well. By and large we have found that a student who can do the job in our transfer program and get his associate degree with us, can do the job in the last two years and get his bachelor's degree.

The national experience is about the same even though it ought to be pointed out that, like any type of college, community colleges are uneven as to quality. Some are excellent, many are mediocre. The record of transfer students and the attitude of nearby universities is one good measure (but only one) of the quality of any single community college. It is interesting, though, to observe how consistent the national experience has been in respect to transfers. A study financed by the United States Office of

Education involving more than 7,000 transfers from 345 two-year colleges to forty-one four-year institutions in ten states was carried out from 1961 through 1964 by Dorothy M. Knoell and Leland L. Medsker.[3] It showed that less than 15 per cent of the transfers had a serious problem with transfer of credits and that the transfers had only slightly lower grades than their junior and senior classmates who had attended the four-year institutions right after high school. Projections indicated that 75 to 80 per cent of the transfers would attain the bachelor's degree on schedule and that of the remainder, less than half had been dismissed for academic failure. The study shows, by the way, that it is best for the community college student to attend the full two years and then transfer, rather than transferring after one year. His chances for success are 75 per cent better if he stays two years at the community college than if he stays only one year.

How do the four-year institutions feel about the new community colleges? The state universities are by and large delighted to delegate the task of screening large numbers of freshmen and sophomores so that they can concentrate most of their energies on upper-division and graduate education. The University of Massachusetts could hardly have been more helpful to us in this transfer business. They see us as their "feeders." They are cooperating with the community colleges in Massachusetts by planning ahead to reserve space for our projected juniors. Each student we have recommended from Berkshire Community College to the University of Massachusetts

---

[3] Dorothy M. Knoell and Leland L. Medsker, *Factors Affecting Performance of Transfer Students from Two- to Four-Year Colleges: With Implications for Coordination and Articulation*, Cooperative Research Project No. 1133; and *Articulation Between Two-Year and Four-Year Colleges*, Cooperative Research Project No. 2167 (University of California, Berkeley, 1964).

has been accepted there. Many of the students from our Massachusetts community colleges are also transferring to the ten Massachusetts state colleges and that, too, is a pattern which will continue as we start to produce thousands rather than hundreds of graduates each year. On the campuses of the University of California there are twice as many juniors and seniors as freshmen and sophomores. In Florida, as I indicated earlier, new state universities are not admitting *any* freshmen or sophomores. Their students will all be community college transfers. Even in the Northeast, the bastion of private education, the private four-year institutions are beginning to demonstrate an awareness of the public community college. Dean of Admissions Eugene S. Wilson of Amherst College has announced that Amherst is actively seeking applications from fifty transfers from junior and community colleges each year. In a talk which he gave recently entitled "Thar's Gold in Them Thar Hills," Dean Wilson said that about the only positive comments he gets from Amherst faculty are on the quality of transfers from two-year colleges. (Faculty rarely say nice things to admissions officers!) A number of students from Berkshire have already transferred to Amherst, Williams, Mount Holyoke, and many other "prestige" institutions. (After all, it was a shorter time ago than most of us keep in mind that the "prestige" institutions were admitting many "average" students who now find most doors closed to them except the community college.)

In addition to the transfer program, the typical community college has a variety of career and adult programs. It is the combination of these three programs that make the community college a uniquely comprehensive and flexible kind of higher educational institution.

By and large the transfer programs are for people in

the upper 25 per cent of the high school graduating classes as to academic aptitude. By and large the career programs are for the middle 50 per cent of the high school graduating group. A low-cost community college with a wide variety of career programs plus the transfer program can offer universal opportunity for education after high school for all but the very low aptitude student. The wide variety of offerings, combined with the low cost, is the key, because one program or another will appeal to nearly everyone in a very wide spectrum of high school graduates. The variety must include clusters of career programs which are diverse not only in *kinds* of courses but in *levels* of courses. Norman C. Harris of the University of Michigan in his recent book, *Technical Education in the Junior College/ New Programs for New Jobs*,[4] talks about this "middle 50 per cent" of high school graduates which community colleges ought to serve through programs characterized by diversity rather than by sheer intellectuality. For example, Harris says community colleges should have a cluster of programs in the engineering and technical fields, ranging from the first two years of a transfer engineering program at the top end of the scale of intellectuality and abstraction, all the way to courses for highly skilled technicians at the other end of the scale, where practicality is essential and where the students are not intellectually equipped to handle very abstract work. At all levels, though, the program must have a solid core of general education or liberal arts courses in addition to the "skill" courses.

The existence of this variety of career programs combined with the transfer program means that there can be mobility from one program to another with a minimum

[4] Norman C. Harris, *Technical Education in the Junior College/ New Programs for New Jobs*, American Association of Junior Colleges (Washington, D.C., 1964).

of cost, time, and effort. Of course, an "open door" admissions policy need not mean a student may be admitted to any program. On the contrary, admission into the associate-degree nursing program or into an engineering technology program, for example, may be quite selective. If the student has been accepted in the transfer program but shows himself unable to handle that level of abstraction, he may with counseling be persuaded to move into a less abstract, less academically demanding program. If he has, for example, been doing poorly in an engineering transfer program, he may be persuaded to shift to a technology program where the mathematics and physics requirements are less rigorous. Or, discouraged with the whole engineering and technology world by his failure, he may shift to a career program in business with a concentration on bookkeeping and accounting. If on the other hand a young lady has matriculated in an executive secretarial program and finds she's really fired up by the elective course she'd had in art and shows herself capable of being a bachelor's degree candidate, she may with counseling move over into the transfer program and plan to major in art after she becomes a junior in a four-year institution. These shifts take place all along the line. Some time and money may be lost by the student, of course, but not nearly as much as might be the case if he had gone to a residential college only to find his plans had changed. How many of us were sure at eighteen of what we wanted to do with our lives?

It is important to expose students to different career possibilities. Grant Venn in his *Man, Education and Work*[5] points out that today's child, unlike his grandparents, grows up in a world where he never sees people

[5] Grant Venn, *Man, Education and Work*, American Council on Education (Washington, D.C., 1964).

doing the jobs which he might be most intrigued with and best qualified to do. He never sees the electrical technician, say, or the low-temperature specialist at work. As a result, "job selection in the technological work world has become a desperate affair, often subject to wildest chance and equally often unrelated to the young job seeker's aptitudes and abilities." [6] Exposure to alternative career programs in a community college combined with both opportunity and career guidance makes the transition into the world of work more rational.

Community colleges have handled in various ways the diversity of their student bodies which comes from this multiplicity of programs. Some have several "tracks" in their English and social science courses, for example. The transfer students will take one English composition course which is comparable to the freshman "Comp" course offered at the four-year colleges and the career students will take a less rigorous course for which transfer credit cannot necessarily be expected by the student. These institutions feel that this multi-track system is the only way to handle the spread in aptitudes without penalizing the brightest students, getting the slower students in over their heads, and creating an impossible job for the teacher.

Other community college people feel that to put students into tracks of this sort is "playing God." English composition is English composition, say they, and to call it "communications arts" for the career students and to separate them out from their more able classmates is to do no one justice. One long-time community college president said to me, "In the long run, there actually is no such thing as a nontransfer student." What he meant, he explained, was that if you do a follow-up study on your students for a long enough period after they get the two-

[6] *Ibid.*, p. 14

year associate degree in *whatever* program, even the least abstract career program, you'll find that eventually most of them will fight their way through to the bachelor's degree. It may be fifteen years later and entirely in evening courses somewhere, but they'll get it. If they have the combination of curiosity, brains, and drive, in whatever mix, to complete the first two years, then they can and will eventually complete the last two somewhere. And so, he argues, it just isn't fair to limit a student's future mobility by putting him into separate track courses clearly labeled "nontransfer." Some institution somewhere may accept those courses for transfer anyway, but by this labeling you are limiting the students' choices in an unfair way. That president ran a college with an open door admissions policy and no multiple track programs in English composition or other liberal arts subjects, and he claims it worked.

At Berkshire we have up to this year stayed away from multiple tracks except in the sense that our career or nontransfer business students, for example, take a rudimentary course in business mathematics for which they typically do not request or get transfer credit if they should happen to change plans and transfer. (A few four-year institutions, though, have given credit even for that course, which indicates how punky this matter is.) We have grouped our freshmen in homogeneous English composition sections, but they have all been graded by the same standard. Most "D's" and "F's" have been given in the slowest sections, most "A's" and "B's" in the fastest. Faculty members grade final examinations for sections other than their own to insure a common standard. But the course itself has been the same for all—ditto for literature, psychology, sociology, etc.

Can we at Berkshire hold to this single track arrangement as we introduce more career programs of a less abstract nature? I don't know, but I doubt it. We are absolutely committed to offering more of a "cafeteria of choices" in career programs for the middle 50 per cent of high school graduates, and the pull between these two commitments—to single track liberal arts courses and multiple level career programs—will probably cause us some painful wrenches, as it does on other community college campuses.

But at least we are in the process of grappling with this knotty problem and we recognize that dealing with it effectively is at the heart of our mission—and at the heart of the dilemma which comes from our avowed multi-purposeness. Multi-purpose institutions always have problems which stem directly from their nature and the community college is no exception.

Our faculty is presently reviewing ways to be more flexible so that our attrition rate can be reduced. We want to "salvage" more students who are failing now. We feel we have probably been too rigid up to this point in our effort to establish a reputation as a place where hard work is expected. In addition to undertaking a careful review of the multi-track possibility, we have initiated one program which we've called "TLC" for "The Last Chance" or "Tender Loving Care." We selected about fifty students who had flunked out but whose test records showed they clearly ought to be able to handle the courses in the programs in which they had enrolled. We asked them if they would like to volunteer for a one-semester program in which they would be required to study for a certain number of hours each day (two hours for every class hour) under a volunteer faculty member's watchful eye in a room especially set aside for "TLC." If they brought their grades up to the required level they could stay in college the second semester—on their own. Thirty-seven students volunteered. There was no difficulty finding faculty who were glad to take part in the experimental program.

Of the thirty-seven, seventeen, or just under half, brought their grades up enough to stay with us second semester. Of those seventeen, nine, or again just about half, also did well on their lonely own in the second semester. There were a few dramatic successes; the program clearly made the difference for a few students. As is often the case with this kind of program, the most important ingredient for these students may simply have been that we cared enough about them to put in this extra time with them. We paid attention to them at a time when they happened to be ready to respond. For most of them, the same kind of extra attention had no doubt been paid them at some points in their primary or secondary schools. But they hadn't been ready to respond, just as they hadn't responded to the normal amount of care and attention we had given them when they first came to Berkshire Community College. Perseverance on our part with them paid off. It may make all the difference in the world for the rest of their lives.

This question of the *timing* of the extra attention is important. It is the reason why it is obtuse to suggest, as some critics of community colleges have done, that funds going to community colleges would be better spent in upgrading high schools. Many youngsters who have taken fire at Berkshire would not have done so earlier no matter how good the high school. They weren't ready. For some reason, they have become ready at nineteen or twenty. The opportunity is there. They seize it.

We had some failures in the Tender Loving Care program, too—three times as many failures as successes, in fact. For those students, our tender loving care didn't "take," any more than had the attention of, say, a particularly sensitive sixth-grade teacher they might have had. Those students may continue to try, if they wish, but it will be in our evening program where they will be much more on their own. For a few of them, *that* will prove to be what they need at this point.

As to the moral of our "Tender Loving Care Experiment," I quote a report of our Dean of Students, who was in charge of it: "Is the program worthwhile? If you have a faculty who will volunteer to proctor T.L.C. study hours, and a study room to spare, you can expect to save one-quarter of your able flunkouts. If you are willing to extend T.L.C. for longer periods, you may save up to half the group. We at Berkshire Community College will, in all probability, rerun T.L.C. in the near future."

The student's attitude is of course critically important. If his attitude is positive, one of these extra-effort programs may be just right. If his attitude is manifestly poor, his chances of success are nil and we either don't accept him in the first place or invite him to leave. But it is the "in-betweener" who is the challenge: the one who *wants* to be interested and to respond to the attention but who may be "hung up," as the students say, after twelve years of boredom with school. Here is where the variety of programs in a community college may make the difference. I think of one student at Berkshire Community College who had been an academic flop from grade school on. Reasonably bright and far from lazy, he just couldn't ever seem to "get with it" in academic subjects. Our Visual Arts program designed to lead to opportunities in design work, decorating, advertising, and commercial illustration, was initiated just as he was tottering on the brink of what might have been a final, disheartening failure. This program piqued his interest and he switched into it from the Liberal Arts Transfer program just in time. He is now doing excellent work. If that career program had not been initiated at Berkshire Community College, he'd be pumping gas at a gas station. He was able to take advantage of a flexibility we have initiated to permit students to shift programs and, in effect, start over again. That is, their previous failures, as in this man's case his "D's" and "F's" in liberal arts transfer program courses, are not counted against him. They will always appear on his college transcript of grades, but his overall cumulative index will not reflect them. Thus he can start with a relatively clean slate.

Won't students abuse this privilege? If we make it too easy for some of them, won't others, seeing the penalty for laziness tempered by second and third chances, continue to duck their responsibility to buckle down? Certainly there is danger in too much leniency. ("Temper mercy with justice" reads a sign in our English faculty office prepared by the head of our English department for his colleagues to reflect on as they grade English themes. The "quote," or "misquote," he took from a freshman's theme.) But experience at other community colleges and at ours indicates that most students will not abuse the privilege of switching programs without serious penalty for past failures. And making switches from one kind of program to another reasonably easy is an essential part of our multi-purposeness in community colleges.

The alternatives to our multi-purpose colleges are just not satisfactory. What are the alternatives? Turn back the clock and *not* expand post–high school offerings in variety and opportunity? Concentrate on more specialized kinds of institutions—area vocational schools and technical institutes which cull out the "hands" students forever from the elite "head" students? Even excellent technical institutes like the one in Erie County, New York, are, after careful study, planning to take transfer students soon and become more comprehensive in their curricula, thus offering their students much more academic mobility as well as the intellectual stimulation of university-bound classmates.

The job that vocational high schools have done over the years in preparing young people for skilled work gives little hope that they can do the job of preparing postsecondary students for an increasingly technical and complex job market. Grant Venn points out, for example, that vocational high schools have been increasing their emphasis on agricultural training at the same time that the number of agricultural jobs has been diminishing dramatically.[7] Further, the idea of preparing a student for one skill as against giving him as broad a base as possible is out of keeping with the times—times of technological revolution, cybernetics, and an accelerating rate of change all across the labor front in ways of doing the nation's work. The proposal to initiate four "colleges" in New York state *exclusively* for short courses in such skills as air conditioning repair ignores two vital considerations: (1) the jobs these graduates will perform tomorrow will change the day after tomorrow and (2) *some* of the students in those colleges might have been sparked to go further than their short-term air conditioning repair course if they had been exposed to other possibilities in a multi-purpose community college.

In addition to transfer and career programs, the third kind of program that contributes to the comprehensive nature of the community college is the continuing education program for adults. In many community colleges

[7] *Ibid.*, p. 74.

the number of adults coming to the campus in the evening to take a course or two exceeds the number of regular full-time day students. Some of these courses are for college credit and some are noncredit courses. Some are full semester courses and some are short courses of three or four weeks' duration. Some of them are "brush-up" courses which adults are encouraged to take previous to enrolling in courses for college credit. Some are professional courses related to the careers of those attending. And some are taken just for the fun of it. The posture of the typical community college is: if enough adults want to take a course and a qualified teacher can be found, we'll offer it. Most community colleges don't worry about whether or not the course should be considered "higher education" or "college level." It is the educational service to the community that counts. If the educational need is there, and the community college is the best place to fill the need, let's do it; let someone else worry about whether or not this makes us less of a "college."

But when the decision is made to offer courses for college credit toward the associate degree, the question of standards *does* become complicated by the fact that it is important to keep evening course standards up to the standards of the day program courses in the same field. Many of our graduates each year have taken at least a few of their courses in the evening program. Many of our evening students will transfer credit to other colleges. So we must be sure that the evening courses are as demanding as the day courses—or as close to it as possible. This is difficult to do if the evening course meets only once a week for three exhausting hours contrasted with three hour-long meetings a week for the day program. Yet three evenings a week for one course is more than many adults are able to give. We have compromised at Berkshire Community College by having our evening program classes meet twice a week. We try to keep our selection of faculty for the evening program as rigorous as to qualifications as our day faculty selection. Many of our full-time day faculty teach one course in the evening. Many also do some teaching in our summer program as well, though we try not to have them take on so much "extra" teaching that they run out of steam.

With transfer, career, and adult education being offered, and with the cultural and intellectual and civic activities carried on at the college, the community college campus often becomes the educational center of the area it serves. The summer programs and the evening programs make the best comprehensive community colleges vital, jumping, stimulating places clear around the calendar and nearly around the clock.

As comprehensive as we are, though, we can't do *everything*; we can't solve the problem of too large a labor force, for example. Secretary of Labor Willard Wirtz is off the mark when he assumes that compulsory education to age eighteen is a reasonable solution to unemployment. Anyone who has dealt with truculent youngsters of fifteen who want "out" of school knows that keeping them there three more years is not the answer to anything. Compulsion in education is effective in inverse proportion to the pupil's age. In some measure a ten-year-old can be forced to learn; it is harder to "make" a fifteen-year-old learn. Having tried to "make" eighteen-year-olds learn in an academic situation, I report that it is impossible. At eighteen there are too many attractions competing for their attention. They are nearly at their maximum power physically. They are old enough to have achieved a large measure of independence, at least under our present society's rules. They are usually social animals at that age, and friendships

—with both sexes—are absorbing. You can't make them do anything as lonely as studying unless they really want to. It has long been obvious as Fred Hechinger of the *New York Times* puts it, that "You can lead a student to college, but you can't make him study."

So compulsory higher education won't work. But universal opportunity for education after high school is another matter. And that is what our community colleges are designed to provide.

One of my teachers wrote on a paper "You have a good clear mind—use it!" and it made me sit back and think. I've never thought about using my mind much but I discovered I have one. I don't know what I'll do with a college education, but I'm beginning to feel right about trying to get one.

A Berkshire Community College Student

4

The Students

Community college students are such a varied group that few generalities about them are useful. Every good community college campus has a smattering of the very bright rebels, some of them rebelling for all the right reasons, some rebels without causes. Terribly serious older students, both men and women; sleepy young men who have not yet matured enough to be accepted at other colleges; well-dressed Ivy League types who have flunked out of highly competitive colleges and are now getting a second chance (some of them will toss this chance away, too); intense foreign students who cannot now afford other colleges which will be glad to get them as proven juniors; these and many more classes of students make up a typical community college student body.

A few general comments on the nature of our student bodies do apply, however. First, the coeducational nature of the community college has definite advantages for its students. At eighteen and above students seem to me to

perform better in classrooms with members of the opposite sex. It's not just that they dress better and wash more
(a minor advantage, surely, but an indicator of their attitude toward their environment and their daily activities);
I think they are more serious and tend to discuss their
classroom experiences out of class more—on dates, over
coffee, or casually in mixed groups in corridors and
lounges. There is less preoccupation with the minutiae of
the adolescent world which each sex individually tends to
get wrapped up in when segregated. A former faculty
member from Berkshire Community College who is now
teaching in a four-year women's college told me he had
trouble adjusting to the teen-age silliness of the young
women in the other college. "They get to giggling like thir-
teen-year-olds," he said. Even though his present institution has a much more selective admissions policy than
Berkshire Community College and even though the freshmen and sophomores there theoretically have juniors and
seniors to look up to, he found less seriousness of purpose
in his classes than at Berkshire Community College. In
men's institutions the segregation tends to foster a different form of teen-age behavior—a kind of tough-guy, know-
it-all, show-me attitude which is often hard for faculty to
break through in order to make an impression on the individual student. And in order to *change* the student,
which I take it is what education is all about, the teacher
must first make an impression. If peer-group standards are
too strong, none but the most impressive and forceful faculty members will be able to crack it in anything like the
measure that would be possible in the more natural atmosphere of a coeducational class. At eighteen and over
young men and women are ready to be together in a variety
of social and learning situations. In contrast, at the age of
thirteen they tend to distract one another in a way that

may be an obstacle to learning. The system of segregating them at that earlier age as is done in England and in some Catholic institutions in this country seems to me to make good educational sense. But at the college age most of them are ready for common learning experiences and, I am persuaded, learn better together.

One disadvantage of coeducation should be mentioned: some bright young women will be reluctant to speak up in class lest they show up the young men. A skillful faculty member can bring them out, but he must work at it. This phenomenon of reticence on the part of bright young women in the presence of men may, by the way, carry over into alumnae life. Novelist Bernard Malamud, who teaches at Bennington College, observed to me that in speaking before Bennington alumnae groups he had been more impressed with the husbands than with the Bennington graduates themselves. One wonders, though, if perhaps these women hadn't caught impressive men by learning to shut up themselves. (Not *all* bright young women have this reluctance to speak up; it has never struck me as a "problem" with my own wife and sisters!)

Students in a comprehensive community college are not likely to develop a snobbish attitude toward others who are less wealthy or less able. In this respect the community college has the same healthy influence on the students that the comprehensive high school has on its younger students, as contrasted with the kinds of influences which more specialized secondary schools like vocational high schools or expensive private schools have on their young students. In the comprehensive community college the academic upper 25 per cent of high school graduates are not split off from the rest of their age group at the critically impessionable age of seventeen and eighteen. The middle 50 per cent are given the benefit of staying with their brightest friends who can set an example for them as the life of the mind begins (or *ought* to begin) to be more important to them all. Where possible, indeed, the middle 50 per cent people are placed in the same classrooms with the upper 25 per cent group so they can interact, though clearly there are certain classes where the brightest students would be unduly held back by their less quick classmates. The comprehensive community college is an essentially democratic institution and the flexibility built into it makes it a kind of microcosm of our society where mobility up or down is determined by performance alone.

Separating all or most of our elite youngsters from those who are less than elite harms both groups. Most adults recognize this potential harm for very young children, but we tend to lose sight of the skewed values that are often formed by separating our eighteen-year-olds into overly rigid compartments. For some eighteen-year-olds, the extraordinarily bright or daring, for example, it may be right and necessary to be separated out. For many others it may be wrong.

There is a growing tendency on the part of highly selective colleges and universities to take fewer chances with students who have problems of any sort. If the applicant has had mental difficulties in high school or if he has a minor speech problem, for example, he is apt to fail to "meet the competition." Max Siegal of Brooklyn College recently expressed concern that fear of the stigma of past psychiatric care may cause parents to delay treatment of their children if they sense that by taking the child to a psychiatrist, they may be limiting the colleges which will accept the future applicant.[1] A friend of mine in the speech department of a prestige college told me recently

[1] Max Siegal, "Mental Illness and College," *New York Times*, January 16, 1966.

that he no longer has to handle minor speech therapy problems as he used to do. "They catch them all over at the admissions office," he said. The result of this admissions selectivity is that the compartments into which we place our eighteen-year-olds tend to become more and more rigid.

Some of the elite eastern colleges, Harvard and Williams, for example, have been attempting to respond to this problem of constantly increasing selectivity which makes the campus an unreal place with little relevance to the world the students will encounter after college. These institutions have been trying to heighten their selectivity by becoming *less* selective—by consciously accepting a few students other than those "best qualified" by their normal admissions criteria. The results so far have been encouraging. But the real democratization force in higher education in the future will probably be the comprehensive community college, especially as our brightest transfer students become increasingly able to be accepted as juniors at the elite four-year colleges and universities and as we maintain an open or semi-open door admissions policy, and low tuition or no tuition.

Community colleges should ideally charge no tuition, like public secondary schools. I am not one who feels as passionately as some of my colleagues do about this, particularly since federal aid programs permit us to give scholarships, loans, and jobs to more and more students. But I *have* observed that every hundred dollars we charge, and every procedure we establish through which a needy student must go in order to qualify for aid, eliminates a certain percentage of the marginally motivated potential students. Even with Berkshire Community College's extremely low tuition of $200 a year, there are each year a certain few students who are not sufficiently fired up about the idea of coming to college to save the money or fill out the family financial status forms to get help. One might say, "If they haven't got even that much motivation, they'd surely fail anyway." My answer is, "True for most but not for all." A few will succeed in spite of all indicators pointing to failure. One man I know who has worked for years in college admissions, both in four-year and community college situations, said to me only semi-facetiously, "The only way to find out if a student can succeed in college is to admit him and see if he succeeds." Here we're faced with the knotty question: how much is it worth to our society to salvage a student with the potential to do post–high school work? Under the definition I am using that would be all but about 25 per cent of high school graduates. Perhaps it would be worth it to our society to offer tuition-free education for two years after high school even if it only meant we would thus salvage 2 per cent of each June's high school graduating classes, making them employable and useful people.

There is nothing quite like outright free tuition. All financial aid programs require *some* red tape, and the student on the fence between going to the community college or "just bumming around for a while" (it sometimes turns out to be for the rest of his life) is simply not the fellow who will go through the red tape. We have federal grant and loan and job money available to students with a minimum of form-filling-out, etc., which goes begging each year because the students who need it won't go to the trouble. Incredible? Perhaps, but how are we going to *change* these eighteen-year-olds and make them more responsible on such matters and others except through education? Setting up *any* obstacles to their continuing their education in a program that just might change them for the better seems to me to be almost like eating our young. Let society pay the tab; let them come to the community college without their having to be very responsible about the process; and then let us on the community college faculty try to build some responsibility into them. That's our job. If we can't do it, we'll bust them out, but our experience shows that even if they only spend a short time at the college before they flunk out we may pique their interest to the point where they'll want to come back and will even be responsible about the process of getting back. This may prove true for them especially as they contrast the "joys" of college with the "joys" of menial work eight hours a day.

Many of our students stay in the geographic area of the community college to work after they graduate. This "holding power" for keeping educated young people in the community is often cited as a major advantage the college provides for its region. A certain continuity is brought to the community in our almost frenetically mobile society. These local alumni tend to retain some association with the college after they graduate. The "community" and "college" aspects blend. I often have trouble distinguishing our alumni from our students. At Berkshire Community College one of our graduates has been directing our choral group on his own time; another helps out with our art displays. Many of our graduates continue on with their education in our evening program. One of the pleasures of community college work is to watch graduates continue to grow. They are wonderfully visible. There are few "town *vs.* gown" problems with us because "gown" is sometimes "town" and "town" is sometimes "gown."

Of the many kinds of students in a community college undergraduate body there is one particularly fascinating group. These are the students of lower middle class or working class families whose cultural backgrounds are severely limited. In any community college there are some of these students, but they are especially noticeable in a new community college in an area where the community college opportunity had not previously been available. They might be termed low-status students. They are first generation college-going people. Their parents could never even have considered college themselves and may feel threatened by the potential change of values and the social mobility that may occur in their children if the children attempt to enter the different, mysterious world which surrounds the word "college." Perhaps most surprising of all, many of these parents do not seem to see a relationship between education and economic success. They may therefore actively discourage college attendance. "We've been supporting you for seventeen years, now go out and earn some money to help out before you start a family of your own!" one girl told me her father had said. Or the opposition may be tacit; the advantages of available jobs may be repeatedly referred to.

Even when the young man or woman persists and comes to college over parental opposition, he or she often feels obligated to pay a stiff weekly rate for room and board at home. Some students thus have to work for money too many hours per week. Some fail academically as a result of this burden their families put on them. Others don't achieve the academic victories they need to stiffen their resolve to stick with it in college. The working hours are usually spent with noncollege people. This, too, tends to make the adjustment to college more difficult.

The college sometimes finds that the parent of this kind of student is an adversary. We are counseling the student to work fewer hours outside the college for remuneration; the parents are directly or indirectly pressing for more. We have enough such students to make it desirable as a general rule to deal directly with the student and not with the parent. Why send grades home addressed to the parent if a failing grade is going to result in a parent's saying, not "You must study harder" but, "See, I told you it was all a waste of time"?

Consider the comments of one Berkshire Community College student on his relationship with his parents and on the problems their values have created for him in his effort to go to college:

> I wish I could talk with my parents about what I'm doing in college. Perhaps they're not interested, but it's more like they're afraid of what I'm learning. They have a pretty rigid view of the world, and they aren't articulate. So we don't talk, because it would end up in a fight or in somebody's being hurt. Some of the kids have had to break completely with their parents but I'm trying not to do that. I still love them, even though I don't want to be like them.
>
> I've been letting all my courses go for several weeks now. I hold a job 35 hours a week, but that's not the reason my work isn't getting done. I reached an impasse. I'm torn between what's really important—work or school. At home I think, "What right do I have to spend all this time going to college?" I feel like a loafer, like I'm turning my back on what life's really like. Then I come here, and it's what I really want. It came to the point where I had to make up my mind how I was going to swing on this. I've been on the verge of quitting school but it suddenly resolved itself the other way. I was trying to write this paper, and it came to me that I don't have to feel guilty about school, or about seeing things differently than my parents. It's settled now. I'll still have to keep the job, but I'll cut down the hours.
>
> My family's been straddling the middle and lower class ever since I can remember. The way it looks to me, my father fell out of the middle class in the depression and we never crawled back up. I'm still sort of straddling the two— knowing I have the intelligence to fit into the middle class, but feeling kind of insecure there. I've been messing around

in college and in the Army and back in college for years now and I still haven't got up the nerve to commit myself to finishing up and living up to the demands of a middle class life. I go just far enough to prove to myself that I could do it, then I quit. What made the difference was getting to know some faculty members here. They built up my confidence but at the same time they kept up their standards. One of them failed me in a course because I didn't turn in the term paper, and it was probably a good thing it happened. I'd kind of thought I could slide into the marks, and the degree, and middle class life without having to admit to myself I was doing it. Everybody's kind of given away the last few points I wouldn't earn myself and said "you made it" but I knew I hadn't. Then came that failure in a course I could have had at least a "B" in, and I finally had to face the fact that you cross the finish line yourself or you admit that you don't want to. Anyway I've made my decision. I can identify with at least a couple of solid middle class people and feel comfortable with them now, so I'm going to make the leap and see what happens.

For students like this one, attempting to move from a world of relatively uneducated family and peers into the world of college people, the temptation to give up trying to communicate with their elders may be even greater than for other college students, as described in Kenneth Keniston's book *The Uncommitted: Alienated Youth in American Society*.[2] Keniston, a Yale psychologist, took a group of uncommitted and alienated college students and tried to find out why they've opted out, why they've given up trying to be on the same wave length with their parents and their teachers. In a nutshell, his explanation is that life in the United States is changing so fast that the world these college students are growing up in seems to them to have no relevance for their elders. They have never really *been* in communication with their elders

[2] Kenneth Keniston, *The Uncommitted: Alienated Youth in American Society* (New York: Harcourt, Brace and World, 1965).

since anything approaching adult attitudes and behavior has been expected of them.

The low-status community college student may be trying to bridge two gaps at once: the generation gap that Keniston describes and the gap between the world of relatively uneducated people and the world of college people. While it is discouraging to see how the deeply ingrained attitudes of these students resulting from their family backgrounds may inhibit their ability to take advantage of the college opportunity, it is enormously gratifying to see some of them "making it" even over the tough obstacle of parental opposition or lack of understanding. Nor is it only parents who fail to understand. These are young people who are really trying to break out of one world and enter another. Their friends, their neighbors, and other relatives are often acting, in direct or subtle ways, against the working class student's groping efforts to break away.

The opposition the nineteen-year-old faces from his noncollege-going peer group is often the hardest to resist, especially for young men. This opposition is rather like the pressure to stay part of the gang rather than get married. One thinks of *Marty*, Paddy Chayevsky's play about the young butcher's dilemma when his peer group friends, as well as his family, look askance at his serious interest in a girl. Unfortunately, for most nineteen-year-olds the drive to get an education lacks some of the primordial urgency which the sex drive has. More nineteen-year-olds' peer groups are successful in pulling them away from academe than from the altar.

One of our students at Berkshire Community College got the most direct kind of pressure from his peer group. When he turned his back on them and started to relate more to the college world than their world, his interest turned to speech and drama. He was cast in a college play. His rejected friends came to the play and threw eggs at him. (They missed.) His disgust at their childishness helped him to turn completely away from their world: he is now doing graduate work.

A sociologist at Berkshire Community College, Marjorie Fallows, has found these low-status students to be a particularly interesting group. She feels there are at least two specific forces acting against them as they encounter the new world of college. The first is their speech pattern. They use varying degrees of nonstandard English, with double negatives, pronoun and verb errors, and lots of localisms. Their speech seems to have been untouched by previous school experience. What has really happened is that they have learned two different English languages—one for school, one for home. The one for school, though, has previously been for very restricted purposes, mostly writing papers for class. The home English was the one they used easily with their friends and with older people they knew. The school English could not be used outside of class without fear of derision. Now, however, in the college environment, they find that the home English with its "he don'ts" and "it ain'ts" is unsatisfactory all the way around, in and out of class, on paper and in speech. Small wonder they fail to speak up in class for fear of being corrected or looking foolish and that they show up less well in written assignments than classmates who have learned only one form of English. Small wonder they tend to be discouraged by the pull between the way they now must be careful to speak if they speak at all at the college and the way they still are expected to speak around their home environment and with their noncollege friends.

The second problem which the low-status student has

in college is caused by his instinctive reaction against involving himself in college life. "Someone else will run things; they did in high school." Getting involved with those who run student affairs is something of which the low-status student is very wary. Typically he is suspicious of those who wield power. His parents have probably led him to believe that people will exploit him if they can and have inculcated in him a passiveness which is often the product of suspicion and cynicism. These students are, of course, somewhat ambivalent, for power and involvement have a certain attraction for most young people, and some of them are lucky enough to learn to question their parents' cynical passivity. For example, one Berkshire Community College student expressed a typically ambivalent attitude this way:

I really liked school through the eighth grade. Then for some reason, I was "advised" to go to vocational high school. I guess it seemed like reasonable advice to my parents. They aren't the kind of people who would question a thing like that, and it just wouldn't have occurred to them that I might have done well in the college course. I was too young to realize that there might have been a choice, though it did occur to me that a friend who hadn't done nearly as well in school as I had took the college course. Not that I didn't learn anything in vocational high school. I learned that I was stupid, and I learned it with a vengeance. They drilled it into us. After that I went in the Marines, and I saw the same kind of thing happening all over again. The boys with the college diplomas would come in and start giving orders to the rest of us—even the old timers with twice their experience and guts. And it kind of hit me, finally, how high a value society puts on education. Without it you don't count. So now I'm back here starting over again to get an education, and most of the time I know it's what I really want. At least I've proved to myself that I have the intelligence for it, but what I sometimes wonder is whether I'll end up using it like so many I've seen—mainly to lord it over the people who don't have it. If that's what education leads to, I don't want it. But I don't want to be like my parents and let people walk all over me either.

That student may make it, but the strain of moving from one world to another can sometimes prove too great even for the intellectually capable student. His ability may be vitiated by the lack of confidence he feels in his new environment. Here is how one bright, low-status student, who had been encouraged by his employer to come to Berkshire Community College, described his dilemma: "My back is to the wall and I'm scared because I'm out of my depth, and not just academically. This is a whole new world here. I don't talk the same language, even. I was top in my class at vocational high school, and I think I'm bright enough to have done college work, but something's getting in the way. I don't belong. If I'm not in class some day, you'll know I couldn't take it any longer." And another young man said this on leaving: "It was an experiment, and I'm glad I made it. Maybe it looks like failure, but I don't look at it that way, or I try not to. Being in college was like having a window on another world and I'm glad that I saw what that other world was. But I *cannot* adapt to it."

Berkshire Community College's Mrs. Fallows refers to the problems which these low-status students face as the "strains of mobility." They must pay a price for their mobility. Often the price is loneliness, for they lose old friends faster than they make new ones in the competitive college world and it is not an easy business to estrange oneself from one's parents and siblings, especially when one is still living with them. For these students the college opportunity has been sharply limited by their class background. Those who make the breakthrough have overcome obstacles that most of us can't even imagine. Once they've made it, they are very much worth betting on, for almost anything they undertake. The hope is, of course, that *their* children will not have to make such an agonizing breakthrough and that twenty years from now universal opportunity for college will be a reality and not just a nice-sounding phrase even for low-status students whose parents never had the opportunity.

Perhaps the most exciting thing about working and teaching in a community college is observing the amazing change in some of these low-status students. One occasionally has the feeling—a truly breath-stopping sensation —"Why, I have made all the difference to that student!" This experience is a kind of distilled essence of the teacher's normal experience; it is rarely found in quite the same distillation in other colleges or secondary schools. For example, my wife teaches in a prestigious and expensive independent secondary school. While she enjoys the stimulation of working with bright young minds, she rarely sees the dramatic metamorphoses in students at her school that she and I and our associates at Berkshire Community College see in our college students. All her students already *have* a lot in the way of information and knowledge and she adds to it incrementally. In the case of some of our Berkshire Community College students we have the feeling that they have been houses with closed shutters until we and a few others have somehow managed to pry open a shutter or two and let light in. The result is sometimes akin to a miracle. Miracles are wonderful to observe; to participate in them is the almost unimaginable reward we reap.

What usually happens first for these students is that one individual among us manages to move a shutter just a bit. I tell our freshmen they should try hard to make real contact right away with one of us whose course starts to have relevance for him—to grab that handle of relevance and use it as a lever to keep themselves in contact with the rest of us. I explain that there's got to be this genuine contact because, of course, no real education can take place unless teacher and student are *really* getting to one another in the exchange of facts and ideas and attitudes. If the student feels the teacher is on an entirely different wave length that has no relevance for him, the student is just not going to give that teacher the attention that learning from someone else requires. If the faculty member after several efforts feels that the student is so apathetic that one more try is simply beyond him, obviously no teaching is going to take place.

So when some of these students have real success for the first time in their lives, I feel we and they deserve most credit simply for getting in touch and staying in touch with each other. If they can find just one of us to relate to, communication with the rest of the educated adult world sometimes follows naturally and relatively easily.

This, incidentally, is a basic reason why our teachers like teaching in our kind of institution. Berkshire Community College's Mrs. Fallows wrote in an article for the *Wellesley Alumnae Magazine*:

Regardless of all the noble or practical reasons for teaching in a community college, the reason I teach at Berkshire is that I enjoy it. Like others on the faculty, I have long since fallen irrevocably in love with those students sitting in my class. Given the chance to teach at a more rarefied academic level, I would still prefer these youngsters who never before knew that learning could be exciting—that teachers really cared what happened to them. Here are girls who might have gone to Wellesley, to graduate with honors, if their families had lived on the other side of the tracks. Here, too, are students who may still go to Wellesley, or Amherst, or the university near you, as transfer students on scholarship, if they can be caught and taught in time and given a dream.

If we were ever really excited by ideas at Wellesley, if we were ever the disciples of a great professor or in love with a subject, I doubt whether we ever lose this capacity for excitement. We may forget it, but it comes back when we start probing the new developments in our major field again, or see the flash of discovery on a student's face. Wellesley, like other top colleges, provides an attitude toward learning that stays with us, whether we know it or not.

It is this attitude toward learning that is most desperately needed by precisely those students who are swarming to the community colleges now. They want inspiration and guidance in a world where their parents can often give them little help. They need instructors who have themselves found learning exciting and who have compassion as well as knowledge. There are not enough such people to go around, especially since community colleges can seldom attract and hold men from top-ranking colleges, unless at the administrative level, because their courses are largely introductory ones with only a smattering at the second level. Yet these introductory courses can be the most challenging, particularly with these students. Those seventy-five students in my lecture hall—the fifteen in my discussion class which follows—have probably never heard commonplace sociological concepts discussed over the dinner table at home. Indeed, they may come from homes where *nothing* is discussed at the dinner table.

For some, the shock of so many new ideas in so many new courses is too much to take. For others, the shock is of a door swinging open to a marvelous new world. Anyone who wants the chance to test her ingenuity in reaching bright but dormant minds and who is willing to see the students she sparked to go on to get the Ph.D. she did not get, will find the rewards great. The students come back, as we seldom did to Wellesley, to find their teachers and say "thanks." They call to ask for advice or reassurance about the next step in their education, or about jobs. They write to tell of successes, or just to say "You made a difference in my life. I wanted you to know." They never take good teaching for granted, nor do they assume you take their success for granted. They know how touch-and-go it all was—an experiment which would not have succeeded for them without the genuine concern of many people.[3]

Another of our crackerjack women teachers, Clara C. Park, also wrote an article about her experience at Berkshire Community College. An A.B. with a major in Greek from Radcliffe and a master's degree from Michigan, she, like a number of our ablest part-time faculty members, is the wife of a teacher at nearby Williams College. Here is how she concluded her article: "[Like many of our students] . . . I came to the community college *faute de mieux*. Without a Ph.D. or teacher's certificate, with 12 years of baby-tending behind me instead of scholarship, able to teach only part-time, where else could I have found a job? Yet I wouldn't teach anywhere else. I believe that for many of our students, too, the *faute de mieux* has in the event given them something they needed and could have got nowhere else. And that is what a community college is for." [4]

Mrs. Park's effect on many of her students has been phenomenal. Typical is Kathleen Evans who certainly came to Berkshire Community College *faute de mieux*. She is now herself a college teacher and gave the principal address at our last commencement. Of Mrs. Park she said:

Take, for example, my World Literature teacher. It was obvious that the works we were reading had done something to her life. That they had given it meaning. As a result, I felt a genuine sincerity in her proposal that this material would be of value to us. She was not asking us to read these works just as a requirement of the syllabus, but she was tell-

[3] Marjorie Rice Fallows, "Teaching in a Community College," *Wellesley Alumnae Magazine*, March, 1967.
[4] Clara Claiborne Park, "Bringing College to the Student," *The New Englander*, April, 1965.

ing us—through her own example—that they would be relevant and meaningful to our own lives.

What was even greater was that she was not atypical, but representative of the teachers I found here.

Kathy Evans is typical in another way of a kind of student we serve: the able but confused or unmotivated student who may have flunked out or dropped out of another college. We are a kind of second chance (or maybe "The Last Chance") place for many such students. This is the "salvage function" I referred to earlier. This year alone we have with us students who had previously been at a host of other colleges, including Dartmouth, Bennington, Colgate, the University of North Carolina, Bates, and the University of Houston. A number had been at the University of Massachusetts and the Massachusetts four-year state colleges. Our previous experience shows that most of them will get back on their feet, return whence they came, and do well.

The story of Kathy Evans, our alumna commencement speaker, is so typical that it might be interesting to quote its barest outlines here as she told it to our graduates:

When I sat in your place, I hardly heard a word our Commencement speaker said. No reflection on the speaker! It was just that I was too numb with disbelief that I had made it this far.

I had good reason for my disbelief. I was *not* one of those students, who, after voicing great fears of failure on an examination, ends up with the highest grade in the class. Rather, I had managed to timidly slip through my high school education with a spattering of "B"s, a cluster of "C"s, an occasional "D" and an endless series of half concealed yawns.

I had a kind of robot response to my public education. I did what I was told to do, but without curiosity or enthusiasm. I automatically followed my friends into the college preparatory course in high school, reluctantly submitting to the belief that a college education was a dull necessity of life.

So after high school I entered a state teachers' college in pursuit of a degree—for none of the right reasons. I was merely submitting to one of the unquestioned habits of our society and to the promise that a college degree was a ticket to a better job. I found that my college education was limited to the dull distribution and consumption of facts. I began to look upon teachers as glorified gas station attendants who say their only duty is filling the empty tank of our minds. Such an educational approach frightened me in its impersonality. . . . And, I might add, I was more than willing to use my boredom and resentment as an excuse for my failings as a student. Yet, when I looked at the students around me, who seemed quite content with this educational approach, I began to have serious doubts about my own abilities. I retreated more and more from my college experience, supplementing it with longer working hours and a more active social life. At the end of the semester, I was a hair's breadth from academic failure. Rather than *extend* my scholastic mistakes, I decided it would be best to simply drop out of college.

After leaving college, I travelled many roads, each of which led to an ominous detour sign. I had entered a world in which I was putting my worth and earning power to a disheartening test. And both, whichever way I went, were considered to be of minimal value. Selling tickets and candy at a local theatre, serving sandwiches and sodas at a snack bar, and sorting screws in an eyeglass factory were hardly pleasant alternatives to college life.

When Berkshire Community College opened in September of 1960, I looked upon it as a kind of last hope. I was, by now, in a rather desperate situation. Few four-year institutions, within the reaches of my pocketbook, were willing to bank on a shaky academic record. But even if they were, my confidence in my own abilities had been so shattered that I considered my own education a poor and risky investment. I was unwilling to give up my job or to assume the financial burden of attending a residential college. Berkshire gave me another chance by offering low-cost education and by accepting me *in spite* of my poor academic record. Besides, people predicted that Berkshire would be nothing more than a glorified high school—well—I had managed to slip through my high school education. Perhaps, then, at Berkshire I could at least maintain a position of anonymous mediocrity. I hoped for nothing more. My ego had received many a severe jolt in the past year, and any illusions I had about my own abilities had disappeared.

Now you're probably wondering—with good reason—why President O'Connell invited this academic loser here today to be your Commencement speaker. I suppose I should tell you now that after receiving my associate's degree here, I went on to the University of Massachusetts to receive my Bachelor of Arts, *magna cum laude*. I followed this with a Master of Arts degree in English and I am presently teaching at American International College in Springfield.

But these are only external accomplishments. What happened to me at Berkshire went far beyond the reaches of my career—it determined my whole approach to life.

It's difficult to analyze the changes that took place in me at Berkshire. There is a quality of mystery that surrounds my experience here. All I know is that suddenly I was caught up in the excitement of the intellectual life. And please, don't call to mind the image of a seedy, solitary figure hunched over a book in a small, dreary room. There was tremendous activity in my new life—the activity of thought and communication.

More than anyone, my teachers awakened this new response within me. I had never really admired teachers before —if anything, I resented them. It seemed to me that most of them were not committed, but resigned to what they were doing. I used to think of my classes in terms of a kind of three-fold division: teacher—textbook—students. The company we kept in the classroom seemed rigid and forced—unnatural.

But at Berkshire Community College I was in for a new experience. So many of the teachers I found here breathed life into the material being studied, and I was drawn in by their personal commitment to their material. For the first time, I sensed a marvelous integration between life and knowledge—a real union between the teacher and the text.

This is what happened to me. I became so caught up in

these experiences that I completely forgot about my old feelings of insecurity and my belief that the best I could hope for was a position of anonymous mediocrity. Exultant over such experiences I found special meaning in the motto above the stage: "To Travel Hopefully is a Better Thing Than to Arrive." The present was no longer a brutal means to a desired end. It was living and vital. I used to plead: "Oh, just let me make it to the degree. That's all I want." But now I realized that by setting up my degree as an ultimate goal, I had been focusing on a small segment of my life. Beyond that there was so much more room to grow, so much more to know and become.

A community college made the difference for Kathy Evans. And she is passing on the torch. What could be better?

To Travel Hopefully is a Better Thing Than to Arrive.

Robert Louis Stevenson
Motto of Berkshire Community College

5

How to Start
a Community College

Since about fifty community colleges are being started
each year in the United States, it might be in order to set
down a few things we have learned about beginning them.

One thing the Massachusetts experience shows is that
the job can be done successfully even when you break all
the "rules." Twelve institutions have now been started in
eight years. None has had "adequate" time for planning
or for faculty recruiting trips on the part of the president.
None has had adequate administrative staff during the
planning phase nor when the doors were opened to students. None has had a good library when the students
first came. All started in makeshift existing buildings: one
in a former jail, one in a former mental hospital, one in a
former industrial plant. Several of us were lucky enough
to get started in a former school building. In just about
every case renovating work was still going on when the
first freshman class arrived. I have mentioned that Berkshire shared its building the first year with junior high
school students. One sister institution, Quinsigamond

Community College in Worcester, Massachusetts, spent
its first year on the campus of the College of the Holy
Cross, through the kindness of the Jesuit Fathers, while
the community college building was being renovated. Another of our colleges spent the first month holding classes
in church basements until its building was ready.

But I think none of us would now say we should have
waited to open our doors until we were more nearly ready.
That would have meant some young people wouldn't have
gone to any college right after high school. The opportunity would have passed them by and it might never
have come again. The kind of student who comes to a
community college is often on the fence about going to
college at all. Since jobs for eighteen-year-old boys with
no skills at all are hard to find, many young men drift to
a college if it is handy because they don't know what
else to do with themselves. Even so, some take fire once
they get there. Many young women, on the other hand,
would be able to find jobs as salesgirls or junior office
clerks if the college weren't there to present an attractive
and reasonably inexpensive alternative. Because they've
had this conscious choice to make, by the way, the girls
stick better than the boys; their attrition rate is a good
bit lower.

Nor are we in Massachusetts alone in having put together haphazard arrangements in order to start accepting students. In New York City some community college
classes have been held in parked chartered buses. At the
huge new college in Miami, Florida, Miami Dade Junior
College, a couple of years ago I saw large numbers of
students studying in their cars on a hot, hot day because
there was no place under college roofs for them between
classes. A disgraceful situation? Maybe. But the alternative for many of those students would have been not to

attend *any* college after high school. Should Florida officials have held up on opening or expanding Miami Dade Junior College until they were in every respect ready for the students? I think not.

The interesting thing is that the students at Miami Dade Junior College and at our Massachusetts community colleges seem to learn anyway, in spite of the roadblocks that have been thrown in their way by their elders' shortsightedness in not starting early enough to plan for them. Some of them even seem stimulated by the situation. There is a high morale, a kind of "we're all in it together, let's make the best of it" attitude. It seems to snap some students out of the lethargy they have been in since they started school.

This is not to say there are not some students who find the inchoate new college overwhelming and who drop out as a result. Some of them might have stayed in if we had really been ready for them. But it *is* to say that those communities which clearly need additional higher educational opportunities for students should go ahead and start community colleges and not wait for elaborate surveys to show what programs should be offered. *Carpe Diem*, seize the day, has been our byword at Berkshire and I recommend it.

We got our green light to start Berkshire Community College in April of 1960 and opened the following September with our 150 students. To illustrate what I've been saying, I know most of those 150 students wouldn't have gone to college at all that September if we hadn't opened our doors. A number of them who probably *never* would have gone to college are now completing their graduate work. Several like Kathy Evans have master's degrees and are now teaching.

The first spring and summer we recruited part and full-time faculty and staff, spent about a quarter of a million dollars renovating our old high school building, and put together curricula for three programs we *knew* the community needed (liberal arts transfer, executive secretarial, and electrical technology; there's no need to start with a whole array of programs—indeed, there are advantages to beginning with just a manageable few). We ordered furniture and equipment and books, spoke to assembled high school seniors in each of the twelve area high schools about our new college and interviewed those who wanted to apply, and planned a dignified formal opening ceremony. It was a rather hectic time, but we were calmly assured by friends from sister institutions in New York state who had been through the process that the job could be done.

One thing we *didn't* do was to let the problems of building any one leg of the three-legged stool of education—personnel, program, or plant—delay the building of the other two. We didn't wait for a biology teacher to come onto the job before we planned a biology laboratory and ordered microscopes and supplies based on a course outline put together by a friendly Boston University professor of biology. There was no time to wait. The result was some lost motion, some unused supplies, some renovation mistakes. The surprising thing, though, was how well it all went, how little waste there turned out to be. It was in a way rather like wartime. One didn't know how much one could accomplish under "impossible" limitations until one tried.

Personnel are obviously more important in a college than programs or plant. So that was where I put most of my attention that April after my own appointment to head the new "pilot" college. I had to make decisions faster on appointments than I liked, and I didn't have time to go and see prospective faculty people. I had to insist that they come to see me—at their own expense. Not an ideal arrangement, but one we've had by and large to follow since, too. Our state travel allowance has never been large enough for me or our Dean of Faculty to do much traveling to interview potential teachers. We've had to rely on our own attractiveness as a new institution, starting from scratch, to lure good people to us. Again, the encouraging thing is that we *did* lure them and continue to do so.

The opportunity to start something new has a lot of appeal and the new college can capitalize on that appeal. The chance to build an institution that will probably endure long after the builders are dust stirs something pretty deep in people. It captivates the imagination of even more people than I would have thought. It permitted me to keep my sights very high as to the calibre of people I appointed, at the outset and since. Each year since we've started we've had faculty applications from just about every state of the union and from dozens of foreign countries. Last year we had applications from forty-nine states. When asked about the fiftieth, our Dean of Faculty replied: "I'm afraid the people of Alaska must have heard about our severe Berkshire winters."

What were the qualities I looked for first? Energy and initiative. Obviously starting a college from scratch, especially as quickly as we had to, requires long days and nights of work. I scared off a number of applicants by talking about the hours of work which I anticipated we'd all have to put in for the first year or so. And initiative was, and still is, vital. I couldn't have people who waited for someone to tell them what to do. I had to have a group of "self starters," or we just wouldn't get underway at all, to say nothing of getting underway right.

At least some of these first appointments should be people of real intellectual bite. *All* of them need not have this
quality of mind—which Berkshire Community College
lecture series participant Tom Wicker of the *New York
Times* describes as the "questing, challenging, skeptical,
analytical, toughly fibred mind of the person who thinks
for himself, whose impulse is to reason and whose gift is
to perceive." Indeed, you might never get the institution
off the ground if all the first appointments had too much
bite. But several should possess it if the institution itself
is to include an intellectual thrust from the outset.

Judgment was obviously an important quality on the
part of our first appointees if we were to make as few errors as possible. Some experience related to the job at
hand would help, too. But I put less emphasis on experience than many presidents of new institutions might do.
Specifically, I didn't care if a person had had community
college experience. I had had none myself, but I had confidence that bright, student-oriented people, irrespective
of specific background, would come to sense quickly, as
I was sensing, the importance of what we were doing and
would soon learn *how* to do it.

A good deal of evangelical nonsense has been written
about the junior or community college "movement"
(dreadful phrase). A lot of it has struck me as irrelevant
or worse. An institution as essentially sound as the comprehensive community college needs none of the bogus
emotionalism that seems to surround it. The basic idea
of this kind of institution can and will stand on its own
in the marketplace of educational give and take.

Community college people, I might interject here, have
a paradoxical combination of pride and diffidence. Some-
place in his *Strangers and Brothers* series of novels, C. P.
Snow discusses this fatal combination in the men his

protagonist, Lewis Elliot, has known. These men apparently have all the qualities necessary for success in the "corridors of power" in England. But they fail to reach true distinction because they are at once proud and diffident. When I read this I thought immediately of the touchy pride which our own new institutions display, especially at our own professional gatherings, and the silly lack of confidence we have at other times, especially in our dealings with four-year institutions and universities. I hope the combination doesn't prevent us from becoming all we are capable of being.

To get back to starting a community college, I would stress again the absolutely top priority which should be given to engaging a nucleus of able, energetic, imaginative people right at the outset. It is never more important to bring in first-class administrators and teachers than at the start. This is the *easiest* time to do it, too. For they can be given big chunks of responsibility and told to go at it as they see fit. Only at this time can a President or a Dean of Faculty proclaim to Department Chairmen as follows:

There are no barnacles of tradition or built-in loyalties and antipathies for you to buck, no scars of previous battles for you to be sensitive to, no set curriculum for you to have to labor long to revise—no need to muster votes in order to make the slightest change (President John Dickey of Dartmouth once said to me that the only thing he knew that is harder to do than change a curriculum is to move a cemetery). There are no limitations but your own energy and initiative. You know your field and we don't. Pick your people. Set up your courses. Tell the librarian what books he should order in your discipline. Order the equipment you need. We'll back you up. Go to it.

The appeal of this proposition for ambitious, zestful educators is enormous. The trick is to pick the best of those who are intrigued by the opportunity. If you pick great ones, they'll attract outstanding colleagues. If you miss and pick a mediocre one, he'll bring in mediocre colleagues—if you don't replace him first. For this reason it's a good idea to leave as much flexibility as possible by appointing acting deans and department heads at first. This gives an opportunity to observe them to see if they are the right people in the new situation before the position is officially filled.

I should not like to leave the impression that the Massachusetts way of starting community colleges is ideal. I would be a fool to argue that there is not a good deal to be said for hiring a president more than six months before the college is to open, as was my case and has since been the case for most of my Massachusetts brother presidents. While making the point that a college *can* be opened in six months or less and that some students will thereby come to college who otherwise never will, I must admit that some of our growing pains at Berkshire and at our eleven sister institutions would have been lessened had we all had a year or eighteen months to plan. When there is a highly developed system of colleges, as in California, even more time for planning can be allowed for new colleges. But in New Jersey they have been worrying the problem for years now and they would have done better to plunge in several years ago. Once a system is started, ways will be found to continue it. In most cases, a community college quickly becomes such an asset to elected officials at all levels that it becomes simply political suicide to take a position against the college. Meanwhile, high school graduates are continuing their education. What is it worth to the particular community or state to have 100 of them go on to college who otherwise wouldn't? That is the standard to measure against the advantages of delaying starting a community college—for whatever reason.

When time is short and the need for the college is immediate, there is a real advantage to starting off in renovated, makeshift quarters. Meanwhile the plans for the new campus of the college can be drawn up with care by the faculty and staff, and in some measure by the students as well. Planning an entire campus from a standing start is hard to do. Doing it from the base of an ongoing college provides a sense of continuity and order. And the planning of the permanent campus can do wonders for the morale of the entire college after the euphoria of getting underway may have diminished.

Some community colleges, under the pressure of getting underway quickly, have ignored the importance of ceremony in the life of a new institution. At Berkshire, we thought it essential to have a formal academic ceremony with the governor and other dignitaries present to mark the opening of the college. Not to do so would have been like bringing a child into the world without some formal ceremony such as a baptism. We also have formal convocations each year for our honors students to which we invite an outstanding educator to speak.

Academic institutions have ceremonies for good reasons. The "stripped" nature of the community college in the sense of stress placed on classroom work rather than in residential arrangements and extensive extracurricular activities should not be carried too far, certainly not to the point where ceremonies are given short shrift. The pomp and circumstance of academe are *not* frills. They are the ways a college pays formal attention when something important happens in the life of the institution. The community college ignores ceremony at its peril that it may never be taken seriously, and not to be taken seriously is the ultimate derogation for an institution as it is for a man.

Nor is the name of the new institution a matter that is always given sufficient attention. Naming a college, like naming a child, is vitally important for the future life of both. If the college should serve a region, or a particular part of a metropolitan area, it seems to me to be just right to seek some name that captures the flavor of that region. That is what we have done in Massachusetts. One of our Massachusetts colleges serves a region dominated by a lovely mountain with a charming Indian name, Mount Wachusett. The name Mount Wachusett Community College was a natural. On the other hand, another of our colleges is named for the principal city it serves, Greenfield. That is justified on the ground that Greenfield is one of the most beautiful and evocative words in the language. One is reminded that as Sir John Falstaff died he "babbled of green fields," often cited as among the loveliest phrases in Shakespeare. Cape Cod Community College was a natural name and describes perfectly what that institution is. Mathematical-minded students at Cape Cod Community College sometimes refer to their college as C^4, but then we at Berkshire Community College must suffer with BC^2.

Care, then, has been taken with naming our Massachusetts colleges and it is right that care should be taken.

Attention should be paid also to the selection of some of the "academic trappings" which will make the institution "feel" like a college and which should come to mean a good deal in the future life of the college. They are traditions-to-be and should be developed with thought and sensitivity. Students should be involved wherever possible in the building of these new traditions, some of which are:

1. The selection of a seal of the college. Berkshire Community College's is based on the Berkshire County seal —a road winding through the Berkshire Hills.

2. College colors. Ours are royal blue and olive. To those who think them too "far out" I reply, (a) no other college we know has them, (b) they provide a very contemporary combination, and (c) some of us *do* like them!

3. A symbol. Berkshire Community College's is a falcon. It was selected by the first class of students. While falcons are not the most common of Berkshire birds, they are regular summer visitors and one type of falcon, the kestrel or sparrow hawk, comes pretty close to being a full-time resident. The students felt the falcon to be an appealing, romantic bird, just right for our symbol.

4. A motto. Ours, which Kathy Evans found meaningful, is from Robert Louis Stevenson: "To Travel Hopefully is a Better Thing Than to Arrive." It is a bit long perhaps, but isn't it what higher education is all about? One thinks of Justice Holmes reading Plato at ninety "to improve my mind." The motto is in plain view on the stage of our auditorium where many of our classes are held. If students sit and look at it for two years, they may begin to see the truth it contains. Or, like Kathy Evans, they may remember it later and see the point. If understanding paradox is the beginning of wisdom, constantly exposing our students to our motto might be said to be the educational process in microcosm.

A new college has to put down roots. One way is to establish places in the college that tie to the history of the region. One can use some imagination in naming parts of the campus or rooms for significant figures in the past and in other ways relate its own life as an institution to the place where it is located. We named a meeting room in our college for the leading Berkshire County hero of the Civil War, General William F. Bartlett, and located there a plaster cast of a statue of Bartlett done by famed Berkshire sculptor Daniel Chester French. Our new campus will also have a room named for Bartlett and will certainly have there some recognition of one of the most famous of American literary friendships, that of Herman Melville and Nathaniel Hawthorne. Melville wrote *Moby Dick* and Hawthorne wrote *The House of the Seven Gables* at the same time and within seven miles of each other in the Berkshires. Perhaps we shall name our two most prominent adjoining academic buildings for these two great friends. But the actual naming of the buildings on our new campus is not yet set, for we'll certainly involve our community in that important matter.

The college should by any means that seem appropriate capitalize on the loyalty which the community feels for the place where it is located. Thus it will more quickly become a genuine part of the community. The fact that Berkshire Community College started in an old school building had certain drawbacks, but an important asset was the fact that hundreds and hundreds of people in the community had attended school in our building. They felt an affinity for the place and thus, in some measure, for the college, even before the college proved itself academically. When we were renovating the building several people suggested we remove a prominently placed, old fashioned, ornate plaque commemorating the original opening of the building in 1897. We wouldn't have dreamed of doing so. Thoughtful people in the community cared about that plaque. It contains some fine old family names of our region. Having the plaque has helped us put down roots.

It is obvious that the new college needs to make itself known right from the outset. Someone once said that the worst thing that can be said about a college is "I never heard of it." That is hyperbole, but it is certainly incumbent on a new institution to see to it that people know it exists and what its purposes are. Babies are born crying so that no one will ignore them, for to be ignored could quickly be fatal. So it is with a new college. The new college, like the new baby, is "hard news," to use the newspaperman's argot. One brand new president in Massachusetts casually mentioned to a local reporter that he was planning to interview potential secretaries the next day. The reporter gave this fact such play that next day the president had thirty women on his doorstep—and no secretary to greet them. The college should take advantage of this interest on the part of local newspapers and other media to call attention to itself in a positive way whenever it can. One needn't worry about the negative way; that will take care of itself.

None of the college's constituencies can be ignored: potential students, their parents, high school guidance officers, public officials who control the college's purse strings, potential private donors to the college, potential faculty from the region and elsewhere, four-year institutions to which graduates will wish to transfer, potential employers of career or occupational students, and so on. The college won't have alumni to be concerned with for a few years (nor alumni sons and daughters applying for admission for a bit longer!) but all of the other usual constituencies a college must impress, the new community college must impress also. Nor will all the constituencies be favorably disposed at the outset. For most people, a community college is a new phenomenon and human beings are still suspicious of the new. Is this watered-down education? How can this college do all the things it claims it's going to do? (It can't, at the outset.) Do I want my son or daughter to be a guinea pig in a new maverick-type place? Can students really transfer to four-year colleges and get credit for their work at the community college?

High school teachers and administrators may feel threatened by the college, particularly in a community where there has previously been no college and hence "high" in "high school" has meant "highest." Four-year institutions in the region may fear that the image of what a college is may be skewed by the existence of this new "noncollege." Nearby private colleges and training schools may resent the new community college's potential impact on their enrollment. Nearby residents may resent the college's traffic and parking burdens. Other public agencies, educational and noneducational, may fear that the existence of the new public college will result in smaller slices of the budget pie for all agencies in the government which supports them. The intellectual leaders of the community may take a "show-me" attitude toward the academic respectability of the new institution.

By and large, though, we've found that the new college can expect support from its community. *Most* people will see quickly how much of an asset the college will be. As indicated, most public officials will be more than friendly, especially if they are fully informed about what the college is doing. As politicians know, nothing is as effective as face-to-face talks. College officers in the first years should speak to as many groups as they can. At Berkshire Community College in our first few years, we never turned down an invitation, no matter how remote the group, no matter how small. Chamber of Commerce groups should be told that according to several studies a college means $1,000 spent in the community each year for each student—money that otherwise would be spent elsewhere. Records of other community colleges and their graduates should be cited to everyone who will listen. A "Friends of the Community College" group can be formed to help spread the word. Such a group can marshal the enthusiasm of those who successfully promoted the idea of the college before it was set up. Our "Friends of Berkshire Community College" have been an enormous asset to the college.

The public media should be kept closely apprised of all significant developments at the college—good and bad. Frankness and openness in dealing with them will pay off a thousandfold in the long run. Public media people are often well-educated men and women themselves and they will be the college's strongest supporters if they feel they can trust the college officers they deal with to "give it to me straight."

Community colleges starting today have one important asset which was not usually available when Berkshire Community College started: federal aid. Federal programs which help community colleges have proliferated since 1960. They make a lot of difference. Of most importance are those programs which aid the student directly. Outright grants, loans, and salaries for part-time jobs are available for needy students—and every community college has many such students. These financial aid arrangements have permitted us at Berkshire Community College and at other community colleges to offer opportunities to students who couldn't have come to us even with our very low tuition. Married students or students with parents who require support often need more than a tuition break to make it feasible to attend college.

There are also federal funds available for purchasing teaching equipment and library books and for helping faculty get on with their graduate work while a substitute's salary is paid with federal dollars. The exciting Upward Bound program, which singles out the needy junior high or high school student who has not performed up to his potential and sends him for several summers and winter weekends to a nearby university or independent school campus, will inevitably be preparing students to enter community colleges. The objective of Upward Bound is to bring these underachieving students to a point of readiness for college. Obviously many of them may not become bachelor's degree candidates. Many of them may be excellent candidates for a community college career program. Thus the community college purposes are furthered by this kind of federal program, though that program's specific design is to "turn on" younger students.

Much of the war on poverty of which Upward Bound is a part is designed to help the American Negro to get a better education. The community college should increasingly have a central place in this effort. We should be the Negroes' college, the place where the disadvantaged Negro can come to "catch up"—whether he be twelve years old or thirty-five. (That's right, twelve years old. Berkshire Community College has a tutorial program called "Awareness with Action" in which our students tutor junior high school youngsters, most of them Negroes, after school. It is one of the most exciting things that goes on in our college.)

In the South, it is better by far for the Negro eighteen-year-old to come to an integrated community college after attending newly integrated primary and secondary schools than to return to a segregated situation in a Negro four-year college (in many of which standards may still be very low for a long time to come, unfortunately).

Indeed, the community colleges should increasingly be

experimental laboratories to use federal funds and other "seed money" to try new ways to bring about social change in their communities. Since one major social change which *must* take place in the next decades in America is the real integration of the Negro into our communities, the community college has a natural and important role to play.

Federal dollars are now building community college campuses, too. And this raises the topic of Berkshire Community College's planned new campus, which will cost $10.5 million with nearly $3.5 million coming from the federal government. Before we turn to a discussion of our new campus planning, though, I would like to underscore the importance of a new college's being alert to the opportunities available to it under these federal aid programs. We at Berkshire Community College have seen no encroachment on our own freedom to run our college as we see fit as a result of taking advantage of the federal assistance programs. Built-in provisions in the federal laws for our educational policy to be made by our Board and our faculty are entirely adequate. I take it that opposition to the principle of federal aid to education is becoming as obsolete as the opposition during the earliest days of our republic to federal responsibility for a central defense system. Nevertheless, it may be worth stating my strong opinion that fear of "Washington" should certainly not deter any brand new community college from getting all the help it can from the new federal programs. To neglect to do so would be unfair to the students of the new college. Most jurisdictions responsible for community colleges in any event are simply unable to resist using federal aid even where they must provide some matching funds. As with highway construction, federal dollars will spark the building and upgrading of community colleges in spite of reservations on the part of conservative local or state officials, and a good thing, too.

It should be recognized, though, that it is an extremely demanding task to keep abreast of federal programs and to comply with the procedures necessary to get one's hands on the dollars. Every new college should have a senior college officer who has as one of his principal duties the relations with federal agencies. It will take a good part of his time, if he does it right.

Finally, with respect to the business of starting a community college, I should say that the staff and faculty who start the new community college will have one important thing going for them as they labor to get their fledgling institution underway: they will sense that most of them will never again do anything as important. And this spirit will infect not only the college's own people. When Berkshire's Dean of the Faculty was visiting one of the great state universities in the Midwest to examine some of its exciting new buildings preparatory to our selecting an architect for Berkshire's new campus, one member of the university's faculty showed him around tirelessly. About mid-afternoon, the Dean became a little embarrassed and protested at the amount of time being consumed. His host shook him off saying, "What could I work on that is more important than building your new college?"

This reminds me, in turn, of a story about President Kennedy and his artist friend William Walton. Early in his administration, Kennedy asked Walton's help in connection with the plans for new buildings on either side of Lafayette Park opposite the White House. The job became very time-consuming and, according to Walton, "I would have to go in to see the President so often about it that I apologized once. He said, 'No. I don't mind being interrupted. After all, Lafayette Park may be the only monument I leave.' "

To build *is* satisfying; to build a college may be most satisfying of all.

And this brings us to Berkshire's new campus.

In a college, people are most important, but their performance is most apt to be good if their environment is benign.

Harold Gores, President
Educational Facilities Laboratories

6

The Campus

The campus of the comprehensive community college
should reflect the uniqueness of this kind of educational
institution. It is *not* a four-year residential college. It is *not*
a high school. It is a place where classes are held around
the calendar, twelve months of the year, and around the
clock, from 8 A.M. to 10 P.M. It is a place where disparate
students of different ages and purposes and of both sexes
come together to learn. It is a center for community cultural and intellectual activities. It is a place where hundreds or even thousands of automobiles come every day
and every evening. It is, or should be, a place which
stimulates and entices and prods people into learning.
The campus must be, as architect Ernest Kump once said,
"the best teaching machine."

The campus should reflect the purposes of the college.
It must be a place which enhances the programs of the college and a place where those programs can be readily
carried on by the students, faculty, and staff. It follows
that the campus should be planned by people who are to
carry on these programs. If the faculty (and the students,

95

in the measure they can be involved) don't plan the campus of a new college, a unique opportunity will be missed. The campus won't really be "theirs." And it can be "theirs."

As an example of how one college has proceeded, let me go back and outline how Berkshire Community College formulated its plans for our new campus, now on the drawing board of Benjamin Thompson, head of the architecture department at Harvard. We formed a Berkshire Community College New Campus Committee, composed of Board members, students, faculty, staff, community leaders, and people from other colleges experienced in planning college facilities. We visited dozens of other campuses, read all the latest literature on campus planning and college buildings we could get our hands on, interviewed thirteen architectural firms and selected the one we thought most "right" for us, put together a rather full program of educational specifications, and accepted with gratitude the gift of the City of Pittsfield to the college of a lovely 180-acre site. At every step of the way the planning committee kept the entire college faculty informed and involved.

We had a strong conviction that each step was a critically important one. We felt we should see the best work being done on other campuses. A study of the literature can give one an idea of which new buildings are exciting places and work well, but only by seeing them, "feeling" them, and talking to those who live with them could we sense what *we* wanted and what architects seemed most interesting to us. ("I like to visit a building so I sense if I can kick it. I like a building I can kick," says one knowledgeable friend of mine, reflecting a prejudice I share against many flimsy-feeling contemporary academic buildings.) In our case, a number of our committee, including me, fell in love with the new buildings which Benjamin Thompson has designed at Brandeis University, Williams College, and Phillips Andover Academy. We met Thompson and his associates and found we talked the same language. He was intrigued by our project. We recommended him to appropriate state officials and, to our joy, he was appointed. The point, of course, is not that only this one architect could design a good campus for our community college. Rather, the point is that our entire committee representing all the college's constituencies was involved at all points in this critically important choice.

For the long run, the choice of the architect is possibly the most important one a new community college makes after the choice of the president. If the architect can be made to be genuinely sympathetic to the purposes of the college and can use his art to make the campus an instrument for furthering these purposes, the institution will be on its way.

The cost of hiring a great architect is no higher than the cost for any other architect. Most educational clients of architects don't know this. For public buildings, architects' fees are a fixed percentage of the total project cost. Indeed, the very best architects can *reduce* the cost of the overall job through their knowledge and care. An Ernest Kump or a Benjamin Thompson or an Edward Durrell Stone can bring great distinction to a new community college at no extra cost to the college for their fees. This is not to argue that only "name" architects should be considered for a community college design job. There are obvious advantages to hiring a local firm, from the standpoint of community relations, for example. The point is that while every community college cannot engage a nationally known, "prestige" educator to be its president, any new community college *can* engage a giant in the architectural field to plan its campus because any architect is intrigued with that kind of fresh opportunity to take a new approach to campus design. The advantages of engaging a leading architect should be carefully considered at the time the selection is being made.

The architect himself cannot and should not, however, say what the purposes of the college are. It is the Board, the faculty, and the staff of the college who must decide this and the purposes must be thoughtfully articulated by them for the architects in a program of educational specifications. This point is worth stressing because all too often the busy new community college abrogates its responsibility on this matter and by default the architect makes educational decisions which he has no business making and probably doesn't want to have to make. The process of translating the college's program into a blueprint for the campus is one which must include a constant interchange between the architect and the appropriate college representatives. This interchange is now taking place at Berkshire. Our new campus planning committee divided itself into nine subcommittees: (1) Master Plan (including coordination of component design, use of site, etc.), (2) Theatre and Auditoria, (3) Teaching Facilities (including audio-visual equipment), (4) Extracurricular Activities Facilities (including athletics), (5) Library, (6) Institutional Services and Utilities, (7) Administrative, Guidance, and Health Facilities, (8) Faculty Areas, and (9) Bookstore. The subcommittees then addressed themselves to each of 356 questions in a *Checklist for Community College Planning* published by Rutgers University. (There are other good planning guides. Some of them, including the Rutgers guide, are listed in Appendix A.) The committee then reviewed and refined the responses to each question. The program we presented to the architect was in the form of careful and considered responses to each of the 356 questions. Answering each question forced our committee to focus down hard on just what we wanted our new campus to do, and by elimination, what we could *not*, therefore, expect it to do. We had certain basic perimeters within which we have had to work: for example, classroom facilities for 1,500 students with core facilities to serve 1,800. We were given as a maximum number of total square feet the figure 270,000. Our total "turnkey cost" budget including everything (furniture, equipment, and all fees) cannot exceed $10.5 million, of which, as I have indicated, almost $3.5 million will come from the federal government under the Higher Education Facilities Act of 1963. These figures, then, gave us a guide on what it would be reasonable to program for.

While the program should be thought through carefully before it is presented by the college to the architect, it must not be a rigid document which tells the architect where all the floor plugs must be located. The architect's hands must not be tied to the point where he has no freedom to use his imagination and experience.

There's an extremely delicate balance to be achieved here. On the one extreme there is the approach which some new colleges, busy in the frantic pace of the first few years of getting underway, have resorted to; "You know what we're trying to do," says the president or the board chairman to the newly appointed architect, "you have seen our present inadequate plant and our new site and you have our catalog. Go ahead and draw up some plans for a set of buildings to serve 1,800 students and we'll have a look at them." So the architect either spends a good bit of his time drawing preliminary plans to help the college decide what it really wants and then has to revise them, wasting everyone's time and money, *or* he draws up "preliminary" plans and then resists changing them on the ground that "We just can't make all these fundamental changes now; it's too late; don't you want your new buildings to open on schedule?"

The other extreme is the college which plans its new campus in so much detail, department by department, that at much too early a stage representatives of each discipline begin quarreling about minutiae rather than thinking with the architect about interrelationships of spaces.

Needless to say, most harried new community colleges err on the side of making too few basic program decisions early enough rather than on the side of planning too much in detail.

Before turning to specific examples of planning the buildings, let's consider the location. The long run location of the college is a critically important choice. If the college is to serve the community, it should obviously be accessible to the entire community and its proximity to major highways is a more important consideration than it would be for a four-year liberal arts college which might wish to be relatively isolated. Berkshire Community College is temporarily located right in the center of downtown Pittsfield, Massachusetts. This has real advantages, for we are at the hub of the principal city we serve. Before we decided on our new campus location, we debated very seriously whether we should not attempt to expand on our present central location. We were impressed by the reasoning of the University of Chicago authorities about that institution's obligation not to move out of downtown Chicago—not to "turn its back" on its community. Then we reasoned that, like many community colleges, we are a regional community college and for those we should serve who live outside of Pittsfield we would always be harder to get to and to park near at a downtown location than would be the case outside center city but near major arterial routes. Half our students come from outside Pittsfield, from as far away as thirty miles. About 70 per cent of all our students drive cars to the college daily. So we decided to ask our Pittsfield city fathers to give us a site about three and a half miles from our present downtown site. Their gift of 180 acres means a savings of several million dollars for the college as against taking by eminent domain a large center city area.

But the arguments for center city locations for community colleges are formidable. The new campus for our community college currently serving Boston—Massachusetts Bay Community College—will be located in center city Boston on a site now undergoing urban renewal. There were many proponents for locating the college on the periphery, but in the larger cities the evidence appears conclusive that the community college should not turn its back on the city. Of course, there will eventually be new community colleges or branches of Massachusetts Bay Community College on the periphery of Boston, too. There are eleven community colleges serving the greater Los Angeles area, some downtown, some in the suburbs.

Wherever the college is located, it should plan its own campus to reflect its uniqueness. Each college, like each person, should have its own special distinctness—its own "style." But the community college as a distinct *kind* of college has certain characteristics which should be stressed in the planning of any community college. First, it is a comprehensive multi-purpose college which serves a greater variety of students than do other colleges. It must keep these disparate students apart from one another for certain educational purposes. The student preparing to become a registered nurse must take part of her program apart from other students. The student preparing to become a highly skilled technician in electrical technology must often work separately from the liberal arts student preparing to transfer as a junior to a four-year institution and major in French. The academically weak freshman student who has as yet no idea what he wants to do in college or in life and much of whose first-semester work is in remedial courses in English, reading, and mathematics should be physically set apart much of the time from the highly motivated pre-engineering student. There must be carefully planned places for each of these students to work with other students who have similar plans and problems.

There must also be places, in class and out, where these students all come together easily and naturally. They must not consider themselves psychologically set apart from one another, in the measure that the college can prevent it.

If the student wants to be completely set apart from other students of differing aptitudes and aspirations, then he shouldn't attend the community college. If the bright young woman wishes to share her college experience only with other bright young women, she should try to go to Wellesley or Mills and more power to her. If the prospective secretary wishes to take only skill courses with others of her own motivation, let her go to a business college and more power to *her*. At the comprehensive community college, as at the comprehensive high school, we're going to mix those young women up together every chance we get, except when we know it to be educationally unsound. And we're going to work with our architect to create spaces where they will come together easily with other students (and with faculty as well) as a normal part of their daily activities. There will not be separate facilities for social intercourse for anyone. We want no social stratification between transfer and career students. There must be no snobbish looking down on the "hands" student preparing for a skilled technician job by the "head" student who is working toward a bachelor's degree. Faculty and students of all programs will, in general, take coffee and meals together, have common recreation and extracurricular activities areas. Classrooms will be of varying sizes so that students from differing programs can be brought together for common intellectual experiences. Faculty offices will be interspersed throughout academic areas so they are easy to get to and so that faculty are readily accessible to students of all programs.

The fact that everyone commutes to the college presents a particular challenge in planning the campus. We want to hold students on the campus as long each day as we can, to create "traps" for stirring curiosity about the arts, for example, on the part of students who "couldn't care less" when they first come to the college. There must be a variety of inviting places throughout the campus, indoors and out, where the nonresidential student feels at home to study or to engage in extracurricular activities, to drink coffee with fellow students and faculty members, or just to enjoy being part of a stimulating group of people. The students will never spend as much time with us as we'd like them to do; that's the principal limitation of a commuting institution. But the more inviting and exciting the campus is as a place to stay, the more they will stay and the more we'll be able to stimulate and change them in spite of our nonresidential nature.

I should make clear here that I don't believe the community colleges *should* become residential colleges in spite of the limitations which a commuting college has. I don't think we should become four-year institutions, either. People who don't understand what we are trying to do often say to me, sometimes almost in a whisper, "Your new community colleges are doing a fine job; now when are you going to become *real* colleges with dormitories and four-year programs?" The point is, of course, that we'd not be doing our particular job if we were to become four-year or residential colleges. We'd be more expensive to build and to operate and to attend, thereby vitiating some of our most important advantages. Our two-year career programs would tend to wither up and die if they were part of a four-year college. I usually respond to the whispered question by describing what I would do if I had an extra million dollars for Berkshire Community College this year and absolute freedom to do what I wanted with it. Rather than building dormitory spaces for students who'd like to live in (and there are many) or expanding our programs through four years for students who'd rather stay with us than transfer (and there are even more of these), I'd initiate a set of new two-year career programs to serve an even wider spectrum of area high school graduates than we now can serve. That would really further our purposes; becoming residential or four-year colleges would actually do the contrary.

To return to our uniqueness and the ways in which our campuses should reflect that uniqueness, our "round the clock" adult education and community activities should affect our campus planning. The campus should be a lively place in the evening. Right now, several evenings a week every single room in our present college facility is occupied—some with evening classes, one with a community sketch group, the auditorium-theatre with a civic theatre group rehearsing Strauss's *Die Fledermaus*. On our new campus these activities will be stepped up. The campus must be an attractive place in the evening: well-lit, safe, inviting, easy to get into but with appropriate security arrangements. And since we're an active place throughout the summer months, planning should include facilities that will serve well on hot days and nights, too.

Since there will be so much coming and going, much of it by car, we must have easy access and above all, good parking arrangements. We see our campus with a ring of parking areas, camouflaged by landscaping and shrubbery so a sea of cars doesn't distract the eye from our lovely Berkshire hills. Areas like the theatre that will get particularly heavy evening use by community people should be especially close to adequate parking. We are typical of community colleges in our plan to have nearly as many parking spaces as we shall have full-time students. We plan to have 1,000-plus parking spaces for 1,500 students.

The facilities we include in the campus plan are being influenced by what the community needs. Our community doesn't need a good gymnasium with plenty of seating for basketball games. It does need a good little theatre. We're planning accordingly.

Since community colleges are new, flexible institutions, their campuses should reflect their willingness to experiment. We are institutions where new ideas for audiovisual aids, programmed learning, teaching machines, and learning resource centers should be tried out. We should try bubble construction for athletic facilities and new kinds of artificial indoor turf. At Berkshire Community College we are planning to use all of these ideas. Perhaps the programs in the community college will be modified by the way these new plant facilities turn out to function, but that's all right, too. Maybe the programs will be *better* than anyone else has tried.

Berkshire Community College's most imaginative plant innovation will probably turn out to be our theatre. We have planned a unique 500-seat theatre. During the forenoon it will be heavily scheduled as our largest lecture hall and auditorium. Here we expect to hold evening lectures by visiting speakers and as many community events as we can accommodate. Here too, will be the scene and the means of our drama and music departments' best expression. What is unique about the theatre is that it will combine a traditional proscenium arch stage and an arena or in-the-round playing area in a new way. On the stage proper of the 500-seat lecture hall–proscenium arch theatre there will be sufficient space for a 200-seat arena theatre. The arena seats will be demountable and on-the-spot storage space will be provided for them. Thus the arena theatre will be able to utilize the lighting, traps, and fly-space of the proscenium arch theatre. The arena theatre will not be a second-best, stripped place with minimal facilities, as is usually settled for when the two kinds of spaces are provided.

By combining these two facilities physically, we may combine them theatrically as well. New works could actually be written for this kind of theatre. Not only will it be a stage-within-a-stage, but the possibilities for creating an audience-within-an-audience suggest approaches to staging and directing involving totally new concepts of drama.

And while we try new things, we are free to refrain from taking on some of the ancillary activities that have become canker sores on more established campuses. Our Massachusetts community colleges won't have any Greek letter social fraternities or sororities which on so many campuses have become patently inimical to the college's educational purposes. We won't initiate intercollegiate football to distract us all from what it is we're really trying to accomplish. Our athletic programs will be based on physical education and intramural activities for *all* students, with the emphasis on sports which can be carried on after college: skiing, skating, tennis, golf, badminton and the like. Intercollegiate competition will be supported only when it flows naturally out of the intramural program and when there is student initiative.

At Berkshire, we want to stress our uniqueness further. We're exploring the idea of having an arboretum of the Berkshires where we'd have all the trees, shrubs, plants, and flowers that exist in our area. And we want a symbol of some kind for our new campus. We're thinking of a special carillon. Architect Edward Durrell Stone put a carillon in at one stage of the plans for the new campus of the State University of New York at Albany. When asked about it, he said simply: "Every college should have its bell." Or perhaps we'll feature our Mount Greylock in some way as Ohio State University uses the Olentangy River. Greylock is the highest mountain in Massachusetts and our campus has an imposing view of it. We might even tie in thematically to an exquisite, authentically restored Shaker village several hundred yards south of our new campus. The Shaker tradition is deeply rooted in our region; with its emphasis on unsurpassed workmanship in arts and crafts there might be something just right about a college which stresses career or occupational education tying thematically to it.

The point here is that each college in planning its campus should stress its own special distinctness. Because so many of these colleges are starting, there is a danger that we all might tend to be the same. If we're all peas in a pod, a real opportunity will be missed and we'll all tend to be bland and uninteresting.

Included as Appendix B are some excerpts from Berkshire Community College's program of educational specifications as presented to our architect, Benjamin Thompson. One of our planning committee once referred to this program as "the articulation of our dream." Our program shows some of the ways in which we have tried to make our campus unique and responsive to some of the principles I have outlined. Thompson has done work for many great educational institutions, but he says he thinks our program the most thoughtful and thorough (without being binding) he has had to work with in the sense that (A) it permitted him to understand in depth what we wanted our college to do and to stand for and why, and (B) it has held up well as he and his associates have translated our words into detailed building plans. (Those plans, incidentally, are featured in an article in *Architectural Record,* November 1967, pp. 166–67.) Thompson has had his Harvard graduate students in architecture using our program to develop ideas on community college planning. So it may be worth including some parts of our program at the end of this volume as a kind of guide for sister institutions which will be facing in the future the fascinating challenge of planning an entirely new college.

. . . there is bound to be a certain amount of trouble . . . if
you are president the trouble happens to you.

Archie and Mehitabel
Don Marquis

7

The President

The linchpin of any college is the president. Perhaps we
can learn something useful about the community college
by focusing on its president and his influence.

It is a relatively easy administrative job to run a college.
It is hard to run a really *good* one, and harder still to *improve* a college. It is even easy to start a new college,
though obviously a certain amount of animal energy is
required, but it is enormously difficult to begin building
quality into the institution right at the outset and to
keep on making it better from year to year. My experience is that external incentives are much less pressing
to make a college good and keep improving it than is
the case with a private business where the balance sheet
provides an everyday spur and where there is a tangible
product to be measured, or with a government service department which reports directly to an elected official who
must run on his record of service. Yardsticks for measuring
a college, particulary a new college, are more subtle, and
for the short run they are almost invisible. Getting

twenty-five students into a classroom face to face with a reasonably well-qualified teacher is not a terribly difficult thing to do. But what actually happens in that classroom is a hard product to measure. It takes a long time for slack standards on the part of a college president to show up. The effective college president, no matter what kind of college he runs, must be a self starter, a person who naturally and continually infects the institution with a sense of the importance of high standards. The institution is liable to be in trouble if the president—to borrow from David Riesman—is a tradition-directed or an other-directed person rather than an inner-directed person with his own psychological gyroscope keeping him "on course" in spite of the lack of external measures of success.[1]

Harold Stoke in his book *The American College President*[2] talks about the similarity of the college president's job irrespective of the kind or size of college or university referred to. The most obvious differences are two: first, the difference between the president of the private institution who must spend a lot of his time on fund raising and the president of the public institution who has the less demanding, but possibly more nettlesome, task of "lobbying" for his funds; second, the difference between the president of the residential or dormitory college with all the attendant problems, and the president of the commuting college where most students live at home.

Having observed other presidents of different types of colleges at work, I agree with Stoke's general thesis of the sameness of the college president's task. And I think

[1] David Riesman *et al.*, *The Lonely Crowd, a Study of the Changing American Character* (New Haven, Conn.: Yale University Press, 1950), pp. 10–25.
[2] Harold W. Stoke, *The American College President* (New York: Harper and Row, 1959), p. 1.

the job of running a community college is essentially the same as running a four-year institution with the additional qualification that the community college president doesn't have to worry about the scholarly publication of his faculty; on the other hand he must constantly fight to establish the identity of his institution as a *college*.

There are a number of pressures on him and on the institution to let the community college be something else. There are pressures to become simply a "post-high" secondary school: the common expression "thirteenth and fourteenth grades" typifies this pressure. There are pressures to become simply a revolving door for mixed-up eighteen-year-olds to drift into and transfer out of as quickly as possible without any real impact being made on them by the institution. If you want to see how strong these last pressures are, read *The Open Door College* by Burton R. Clark [3] which describes a new two-year college and its difficulty in establishing itself as a genuine collegiate institution. There are pressures to become simply a training school which makes a gesture in the direction of the liberal arts but which is really looking over its shoulder at industry recruiters interested in hiring trained people and not in "frills" like child psychology or world literature.

Since few people in a community know at first what to expect of a new community college, the easy thing for the president to do is allow the community to end up expecting very little and getting very little in the way of a collegiate institution with its own integrity and identity and intellectual muscle. The influence of secondary schools on community colleges has been strong and in this particular regard it has been negative. Some of the best

[3] Burton R. Clark, *The Open Door College* (New York: McGraw-Hill Book Co., 1960).

teaching in this country is done in public high schools and some of the best community college teachers are people who have moved into community college faculties from public high schools. But one does not expect from a high school the same kind of yeasty, controversial, combustible effect on the community that one has the right to expect from a college. In the measure that the community college president permits his college to become more like a properly conservative high school than like a university or a four-year liberal arts college in its catalytic effect on the cultural and intellectual life of the community it serves—in that measure he has failed to make his college all it really ought to be. And even more important, he has failed to provide his students with the kind of intellectual atmosphere which they are now ready for, which, indeed, they require at eighteen to stretch their minds as far as they should be stretched.

Mr. Charles W. Ingler once described this atmosphere well in an article on Ohio community colleges:

What is the main difference between the public school education and higher education? It is not that one group of teachers is better or worse than the other. It is not that one level of work is more important or more difficult than another. It is not, in all cases, even that one area of study is more advanced than another.

The basic difference is this: that when the student of seventeen to nineteen years of age goes beyond the twelfth grade, he moves into an area of study in which unprovable ideologies and dilemmas begin to appear. It is at this stage that he comes to grips with the questions for which the human race does not yet have conclusive answers, and he now must participate in the pondering of these questions. In his earlier years he was studying descriptions of known facts, for the most part, and during his adolescence we did not want him to lose faith by worrying over imponderable problems. At the college age, however, he is assumed to be ready for the difficult and sometimes discouraging study of both popular and unpopular ideas, as well as facts.[4]

Let me use an example from Berkshire Community College's own experience. Berkshire Community College recently came of age as a college in the eyes of the community we serve—a relatively isolated rural county of 140,000 in Western Massachusetts with one city of 56,000 in which the college is located. The coming of age took place in a storm of controversy which would probably not have occurred in a community where a college had long been established. In our community lives a man named Tenneson who defected to Red China after the Korean War—one of the "infamous 21" American soldiers in Korean prisoner-of-war camps who made the choice at the end of the conflict to go to Communist China rather than return to the United States. Last year, this man was invited to appear before the students of our college to talk about his life in Red China and to participate in a college radio program on the subject of the war in Viet Nam. The defector, an articulate, earnest man who returned to this country a dozen years ago and now holds a responsible job in our community, was known to feel that we are wrong in being at war in Viet Nam, just as in his opinion we were wrong on certain of our policies in Korea.

Local union groups, supported by several community organizations including veterans' groups, were outraged by the invitation to the defector and demanded that it be withdrawn. Their demand was declined by the college and an offer of equal time to present their views on the radio and before the college students was made instead. In-

[4] Charles W. Ingler, "Governing Principles for Policy Toward Community Colleges," *Educational Research Bulletin*, 40 (February 8, 1961), pp. 29–31.

censed that a defector should have a forum, these groups held a stormy demonstration while the radio program was being aired. One of the placards they carried read, "Patriotic American Teachers for our *Children*" (emphasis mine).

It was interesting that so many citizens and citizens' groups in our community would miss the point that a college—if it really is to be a college—must permit all sides of controversial issues to be heard and obviously does not itself necessarily support the views of the speakers to whom it gives a forum. These groups also missed the obvious point that college students are *not* children who must be protected from controversy.

The experience of having Berkshire Community College embroiled in controversy was unquestionably a useful educational one for our students and our community. (I confess, though, I personally had a few sleepless nights as the tension mounted—and it *was* tense. One morning we found red paint on the "Berkshire Community College" of our main college sign. With restraint we ignored the paint and just left it there. Eventually the weather wore it off. But it haunted me.) Countless students and citizens of our community (including one minister) have commented that the experience made them really focus down for the first time on the issues at hand, including the primordial issue of free speech. At the height of the controversy I quoted Justice Holmes's remark that freedom of speech is "freedom for the thought that we hate." It has been quoted back to me a number of times.

What did we learn from the controversy? Well, here is the way I decided to summarize the experience for our graduates at the end of the academic year:

My hope today is that you've learned to ask the tough and searching and sometimes irreverent questions, to examine issues from all standpoints irrespective of how upsetting to yourselves or others that examination may be. Your college has come of age this year in the controversy which surrounded its effort as an institution to provide circumstances under which its students could examine all sides of the toughest questions. You as individuals have come of age intellectually only if you have learned the lesson of that controversy, namely that the search for the right answers is not always a popular or easy business, but that the alternative is to commit the great sin. That sin is to use your minds at something less than full speed or not to use them at all in addressing the vital questions of the day. For a college or for a bright person to refuse to address the tough questions is a form of suicide.

I hope you've each had some good moments here this year and last. Moments, especially, where you've really felt the thrill of using your mind at full speed on something you think important. Let me tell you about *my* best moment this year. It took place subsequent to Mr. Tenneson's appearance at the college when I asked the assembled freshman class if they had questions for me about our controversy. Many of you graduates were also present. It *wasn't* the moment when I was asked if Berkshire Community College might be restricted in the future on speakers who could be brought in and I said, "Not while I am president," and there was applause. That was a bit theatrical. But those of you who were there may recall that another student asked how I personally felt about Mr. Tenneson's negative views on President Johnson's Vietnam policy. When I replied that I thought Mr. Tenneson was dead wrong, I recall a hush while it dawned on many of the students for the first time that I really meant it when I said all sides must be examined openly. I could *feel* the lesson being learned: because if I would go through all that controversy and put Berkshire Community College through all that controversy to bring to this platform and our Berkshire Community College radio program a man whose views I happen to disagree with, I must really have a commitment to truth rather than repose. Last year I quoted Emerson to you: "God offers to everyone his choice between truth and repose. Take which you please, you can never have both." I know better now than I did then how right Emerson was: the search for truth is *not* a reposeful business.

One thing we learned is that nothing stimulates students as much as controversy. This year the college's visiting lecturers include the Korean defector again; a representative of the John Birch Society; and Dr. John Rock, the Catholic gynecologist who is author of the book on birth control entitled *The Time Has Come*[5] (our community is about 70 per cent Roman Catholic, so Dr. Rock's book and his thesis that "the pill" is morally right is an extremely controversial one here). Eyebrows have been raised at each of the speakers, but no placards. Our community and our students are beginning to get the idea that controversial issues are part of the experience of going to college.

It is essential that a community college, just like any institution of higher education, establish its identity as a place where students are exposed to conflicting views and permitted and encouraged to seek the truth for themselves. As long as the community college is timid on matters of this sort, its students will be shortchanged. And in the long run, so will the community, especially if there are no other colleges or universities in the area to provide this kind of forum for free exchange of ideas on all subjects.

There may seem to be an anomaly here in the sense that I earlier was pointing out the ways in which the community college is unique, yet in terms of intellectual freedom I have just been insisting that the community college be considered in just the same category as any other institution of higher education. The answer is that the community college can have *both* the requisite uniqueness in educational programs *and* the essential equality of

[5] John Rock, *The Time Has Come: A Catholic Doctor's Proposals to End the Battle Over Birth Control* (New York: Alfred A. Knopf, Inc., 1963).

status with other institutions of higher education in respect to academic freedom. But nobody will fight to establish this uniqueness and this equality if the community college president does not. Unless he makes abundantly clear that he will fight if necessary for his faculty's right to say what they please and to invite whom they please to speak at the college, the faculty will tend to be timid, and timidity is inimical to higher education as I understand higher education. The *last* thing our community college students need is timid faculty.

The president must try to bring onto his faculty strong men and women who have differing opinions. The bigger the college gets the more chance there is to have people of divergent views in each department. Thus the student is exposed to adults who teach him to think for himself by not agreeing among themselves. Berkshire Community College's smallness has provided thus far an intimate atmosphere that has clearly helped many young students find themselves. But I am glad we are getting large enough now to bring in a sufficient number of forceful, able people who simply by the percentages of numbers hold divergent views from one another on a variety of issues—including, of course, matters directly related to their own disciplines.

The fact that most community college students live at home means that they need the catalytic influence of a strong-minded and abrasive faculty even more than do the students who leave home to attend residential colleges. Why is this so? In the first place, one of the main reasons they have *not* gone away to college is that they are less daring than their peers. There are, of course, many exceptions to this statement but a number of studies have demonstrated that one of the two most pronounced differences between community college students and residential college students is that community college students are less willing to take risks. (The other difference is that they have lower academic aptitudes. This is also to be expected and also subject to many exceptions.)

Second, community college students need the abrasive influence of strong faculty people because they all return each evening to their homes where they are subject to the same family influences they have known all their lives. These influences are often intellectually bland or worse. Thus the students have only part of the day to be exposed to new ways of thinking, to get "fussed up" by challenges to their previous ways of approaching life.

Third, since students in a typical community college are all from the same geographic area and tend to be from the same socio-economic group, their parochial attitudes need to be shaken up by faculty whose backgrounds and views are very different.

To counteract these forces which tend to make our students narrow, our faculties must feel the freedom—indeed, be encouraged—to speak out and make their views known to students. To use a favorite phrase of Justice Holmes, this freedom should be an "inarticulate major premise" of the faculty's day-to-day functioning. Author James MacGregor Burns said to me regarding Berkshire Community College's free speech fight, "If you have to stop and think if you'll get in trouble before you speak out or invite someone else to speak out, then you're already in trouble."

This feeling of freedom is a very nebulous thing. It pervades an institution or it does not. It is a precious thing for a faculty to have and nobody generates it or stifles it in anything like the same measure as the president. Establishing this atmosphere of freedom may be the most important thing a president of a new college can do for his faculty after seeing to it that they get paid. Nurturing this freedom and defending it are perhaps the most important continuing responsibilities a community college president has after recruiting faculty who can use the freedom provocatively and responsibly.

I stress this atmosphere of intellectual freedom because I think it is a crucial matter in which community college administrators have not been as perceptive and bold as we ought to be. And it is a matter which many community college boards of trustees have not thought about or would not agree on if they did think about it. Many community college boards of trustees are locally elected officials. In many places they are the same boards which oversee the operations of the local primary and secondary schools. It is difficult for such a board to see the importance of having their college be a wide-open, free-wheeling institution where some heat is generated as well as lots of light. Isn't it simply a thirteenth- and fourteenth-grade extension of the local high school? The result is that too many community college campuses are places where there hasn't been any healthy controversy for years, if ever. While some of our university friends are perhaps being distracted by *too much* controversy, most of us are lolling in a backwater with too little. In the long run too much is much better than too little.

Recently the American Civil Liberties Union urged that new colleges right from the outset address themselves to the critically important matter of academic freedom. The Civil Liberties Union cited the leisurely pace with which older, established colleges were able to permit "an evolution of the academic spirit" to develop, and contrasted this evolution with the problems attendant on starting new colleges quickly today under the pressures of burgeoning enrollment. The CLU stated: "Now maturity must be achieved overnight if the new college is to leave an imprint of intellectual integrity on the thousands of students who will crowd its campuses in the next few years." [6]

New two-year colleges are even less apt to create from the start a climate of openness and freedom than new four-year institutions. We have, after all, lots to do in starting community colleges and usually we have less time to plan than do new four-year institutions. Many of us are working so hard just to handle the nuts and bolts tasks in our growing colleges that it never occurs to us to examine the climate of academic freedom on our campuses. And if it does occur to us, our reaction is liable to be: "I have enough problems right now, thank you, without asking for new problems which intellectual controversy brings," or, "My community relations are important to me and to my college. Why should I encourage my faculty to make people mad at us?"

But without a climate of openness and freedom the faculty cannot be expected to reach the intellectual "critical mass" that will excite students and teach them to think for themselves.

In Massachusetts we are fortunate because the community colleges are controlled by a state board, removed from the pressures of local politics which are apt to inhibit the development of real academic freedom. It was fortuitous that our system was set up this way; it was simply because local jurisdictions in Massachusetts do not have funds to contribute to the operation of the community colleges. Their poverty in turn is due to an antediluvian system of state aid to cities and towns for local schools. So in spite of high property taxes, local jurisdictions can't help pay the way for the community

* *New York Times*, November 21, 1965.

colleges and thus were not given a voice in the actual operations of the colleges. An unplanned for and salutary result is that we have a high-minded and statesmanlike community college board responsible for policy at all the state two-year colleges. This board, appointed by the governor, is under no pressure from voters in the local communities who might tend to be myopic on matters related to academic freedom. Hence the board has left the colleges free to establish their own identities in their communities. Within the broadest possible guidelines, formulation of educational policies, including those related to who should be invited to speak at the colleges, has resided with the college presidents and their faculties. That is where it ought to be, of course, if the institutions are to be true colleges.

I should add that each Massachusetts community college has a local advisory board which serves as a useful liaison with the community. Because those boards are also appointed by the governor, they too are inclined to be insulated from the more petty aspects of local politics. Thus they have been helpful and not officious. The Berkshire Community College Advisory Board, chaired by Millicent McIntosh, President Emeritus of Barnard College, voiced its strong support of our academic freedom in the recent controversy. Professor James MacGregor Burns of Williams College, referred to earlier, was at that time a member of this board.

It must be difficult for the new community college to develop the kind of collegiate identity I am discussing in a community where the superintendent of schools exercises absolute authority over the college president. I know of one college where the superintendent moves faculty into the college from the elementary or secondary schools and back at will. The president has next to nothing to say about faculty appointments. My guess is that under such circumstances the community college never *can* become the kind of institution of higher education I am discussing here. This is not to say, though, that local policy formulation precludes the development of a college in fact as well as in name. But it is to say that it takes a rare restraint on the part of local officials to let it develop so. And, above all, it takes a president who *insists* that his college be given the freedom to develop so.

How much, in turn, the faculty itself ought to be involved in the educational policy making of the college, as well as in the great grey area of budget and personnel policy, is a matter which I don't intend to treat at length here. Suffice it to say that the more basic decisions regarding how much the faculty *should* be involved ought to be made by their president and their Dean of Faculty, operating under general guidelines established by the board of trustees. Certainly, too, there should be as much autonomy from other governmental agencies as can be attained.

President James Perkins of Cornell has recently spoken out against university faculties being so much involved in educational policy making that they may forget that their primary jobs are the acquisition, transmission, and application of knowledge.[7] I am inclined to agree that his may be the right caution with respect to universities and to add that if community colleges are to be flexible and responsive to the changing needs of their communities, too much faculty policy making may cause problems. Faculties may tend to be too conservative to be willing to change educational policies or programs as easily and rapidly as necessary in a community college. If they are

[7] James A. Perkins, *The University in Transition* (Princeton: Princeton University Press, 1966), pp. 53–55.

too deeply committed to conventional liberal arts education they may not be willing to initiate new career or occupational programs. They may feel threatened by talk of multi-tracks—of the need for offering several levels of introductory courses in their disciplines, including less abstract ones than the "transfer" courses. On the other side of the question, most new community college faculties need to feel they are in a college environment, and a measure—usually a large measure—of faculty participation in educational policy is the norm in most college and university faculties. It is the president who must balance these two counter pressures. He must be out in front to change the college to respond to changing needs, yet he should carry his faculty, as well as his board, with him or the changes won't really be put into effect. A curriculum, after all, is what goes on in the classrooms, not what is written in a catalog. Administrators' fiats notwithstanding, the faculty determines what really goes on in the classrooms. (And if they don't, what happens in the classrooms is *certainly* not going to have any intellectual bite!)

The community college president must be especially sensitive to this need of his faculty to feel like a genuine college faculty. In addition to intellectual freedom, they must therefore be given a reasonable amount of power in matters of budget, personnel, and educational policy making. The definition of "reasonable" will differ from college to college and state to state, but unless the president fights for his faculty's rights in these matters, no one will. A college run entirely by decrees from the board or superintendent, or the president himself, will never develop into a viable institution to compare with the liberal arts college or the university. And the community college student will be the loser.

My guess is that the faculty of Berkshire Community

College has about two-thirds as much real power in educational policy and faculty personnel matters as the faculty of Dartmouth College, with which I am familiar. Maybe that is the way the relative powers ought to be.

To come to the president himself, what kind of bird should the community college president be? If he is starting a college, and many community college presidents have that as their first task, he should obviously be a person of energy. Perhaps that is the first requisite anyway. Many experienced executives, like Chester Barnard, former President of New Jersey Bell Telephone Company, feel that vitality is the number one quality for any executive to have. So probably a new community college should have a reasonably young president. One recent study[8] showed that newly appointed community college presidents are getting older. Why? Because selection committees are getting more conservative? One would somehow expect the trend to be the other way.

The community college president must obviously be a person of some judgment and be able to get on with people in the community. It is axiomatic, too, that he must be able to delegate authority. As I mentioned earlier, he should be the kind of person who is a self starter, who periodically asks himself the searching question, "Am I running my job or is my job running me?" Henry Wriston, former President of Brown University, discusses this question in his book, *Academic Procession: Reflections of a College President*,[9] the wisest book I know on academic administration. Wriston refers to the paradox of a busy college president's dealing first thing in the morning with

[8] Raymond E. Schultz, "Changing Profile of the Junior College President," *Junior College Journal*, October, 1965.
[9] Henry Wriston, *Academic Procession: Reflections of a College President* (New York: Columbia University Press, 1959), pp. 157–58.

the mail that comes in. Why, he asks, should the president's freshest hours be spent dealing with what someone *else* thinks is important? Rather, if he's worth his salt, he has himself thought of things since he left his desk that require his attention first thing the next morning. Some of the weakest college administrators I know are people who deal very well with things coming at them. They never control their own destinies, though, by deciding for themselves what they'll turn their attention to next. They let the matter be decided by whoever next comes in the door or whatever piece of paper their secretaries next bring to them.

The community college president should be an innovator. If ever there was a place to try new ways to educate college students, it is in the new community college. But B. Lamar Johnson of the University of California in a recent nation-wide study of experiments in two-year colleges[10] found very little to report. Why are we not doing more? Mostly because it's easier to ape the four-year institutions in our transfer programs and to follow the other community colleges and industry's conservative suggestions in new career program offerings. On the first point, sometimes there's a problem of transferring credit for "experimental courses." We have a kind of innovation at Berkshire Community College—a class which I give, once a week, for all freshmen. I devote the first semester to "The Arts" and the second semester to "Public Affairs." We have concerts, Shakespearean performances, poetry readings, discussions, and lectures; some are by me, some by people I bring in. This was the class which Tenneson, the Korean defector, addressed. The freshmen write several themes about the sessions. These are graded by their

[10] B. Lamar Johnson, "Islands of Innovation," Occasional Report No. 5, UCLA Junior College Leadership Program, 1964.

English composition teachers. The course gives all the freshmen a common intellectual experience irrespective of their program, and it gives them something to write about, a problem for many freshmen in all kinds of colleges. During the second semester they are responsible for the contents of the front page and editorials in our excellent local paper, *The Berkshire Eagle,* and are examined on the contents. The course provides one credit for each semester and is a requirement for graduation with an associate degree. It is a reasonably demanding course. Yet I have not been able to convince the University of Massachusetts, which has been wonderfully cooperative with our community college in every single other respect, to give transfer credit for it, and our many students who transfer over there are penalized, in effect. The usefulness of the course is thus somewhat limited by its "nontransfer" status. This is one example of why innovation is tough. But, of course, it is no excuse for not continuing to try.

For the community college president to be an intellectual person may be vitally important in setting the tone for a new community college or for improving the tone of an established one. By intellectual, I mean a person who delights in the play of the mind over a wide range of thought and who reads widely to feed this appetite. The chief distinction between community college presidents and four-year college and university presidents I have known is that many more of the latter are what I would term intellectuals. Community college boards, looking above all for responsible men whom they won't have to worry about, are apt to think of intellectuality as a very secondary desideratum. Yet for a new young college an intellectual president can provide a kind of institutional curiosity and a respect for the life of the mind that can infect the institution in no other way.

There is an interesting paradox here. Many community college boards feel the president should hold a doctorate. That is a laudable goal. The best community college president Massachusetts has had, in my view, was a Ph.D. in history from Brown University who came to his presidency from a teaching post at the Massachusetts Institute of Technology. His intellectuality had effects on his college, almost by osmosis, that I am sure will be felt for decades to come. (Unfortunately for us, he left his community college presidency after three years to head a university history department. One of his university colleagues commented on his accepting this position in "real" academe, "Congratulations on your re-entry.") One of the yeastiest and most intellectually stimulating community college presidents I have known was a Ph.D. from Yale, the late Lawrence L. Bethel of the Fashion Institute of Technology in New York City, an excellent community college which emphasizes career programs of a nature indicated in its title. One could sense the effect of the qualities of his mind on his colleagues and students at his two-year college.

The trouble is, though, that too often insisting on the doctorate means the college is headed by a Doctor of Education. Perhaps I haven't been looking in the right places, but I have not found very many Ed.D. holders who are real intellectuals. Messrs. Conant[11] and Koerner,[12] in their books on teacher-training institutions, explain why this is so: the dry-as-dust methods courses tend

[11] James Bryant Conant, *The Education of American Teachers* (New York: McGraw-Hill Book Co., 1963).
[12] James D. Koerner, *The Miseducation of American Teachers* (Boston: Houghton Mifflin Co., 1963).

to drive out the intellectually inclined students before the doctorate is reached. I needn't elaborate on this here except to say that while those teacher-training institutions are certainly changing for the better, it will be some time before the products of their doctorate programs will reflect the changes in a significant measure.

I would go further and say that community college boards have in general been too conservative in making what is incomparably their most important decision: the choice of the community college president. (The thrust of John O'Hara's perceptive novel of academe, *Elizabeth Appleton*,[13] is that this choice is in reality the *only* important decision a college board of trustees makes. Hence in the novel the board declines to select the obvious candidate simply because he is so obvious a choice that to pick him would be to let their only decision be made for them by exterior forces.) For a community college board of trustees to pick a secondary school educationist because he obviously knows the ABC's of educational administration may, of course, result in a smooth-running community college, but it may be bland and colorless, as well. Actually, the fundamentals of educational administration are not all that abstruse. A generalist executive who is bright and curious can learn them in six months— and if he's a good generalist he'll know how to get expert help in the interim. One of our Massachusetts community college presidents is a former railroad executive; another is a former Dean of Men in a large private university. Neither holds a doctorate. They are both extremely effective presidents. In short, good college presidents are where you find them, just as good cabinet members or good Peace Corps administrators are. By and large you

[13] John O'Hara, *Elizabeth Appleton* (New York: Random House, Inc., 1963).

have to go and seek them out. Waiting for them to apply for the job is not the best way to get them. Yet that is how many, if not most, present community college presidents (including me) were recruited. Perhaps that's why we're not better than we are.

A common shibboleth concerning college presidents is that they must "belong to the students" or be "for the students." Lists of desiderata of committees looking for presidents are sometimes headed by a phrase to the effect that what is sought is a man who will be student-oriented, who will see his job as being primarily to serve the students, to be aware of their needs and to spend his time seeing to them. This is patent nonsense. It is nearly as naive as the position of the "new breed" in our universities who view students as victimized by faculty and administrators and who would have the president erase all distinctions and turn the institution over to an unorganized spontaneous brotherhood of students, and perhaps passersby, seeking beauty and truth. While colleges are not box factories or military camps and must be run very differently from other organizations, the answer to student problems is not anarchy. Nor is the answer a paternalistic or avuncular president. Not even the president of a community college, without responsibility for overseeing student residences or research activities or for fund raising, can be primarily the students' man. If he is to be successful he must be too many things all at the same time to too many other constituencies of the college: faculty, trustees, alumni, secondary school and university representatives, colleagues in other agencies of government including legislators, to mention a few. He cannot focus a disproportionate amount of his own time and energy on the students or he'll slip in his supporting of his faculty and his student counselors. It is *they* who must make students their main concern—and who are in turn dependent on the president for protection and support that only he can provide. It is they, too, who must make the decisions about students. If the president gets too involved in student affairs he will inevitably start making decisions about students which somebody else on the college staff should make. This is a cardinal sin for any executive. It might be worth quoting here Chester Barnard's wonderfully perceptive comment on "not deciding."

> *The fine art of executive decision consists in not deciding questions that are not now pertinent, in not deciding prematurely, in not making decisions that cannot be made effective, and in not making decisions that others should make.* Not to decide questions that are not pertinent at the time is uncommon good sense, though to raise them may be uncommon perspicacity. Not to decide questions prematurely is to refuse commitment of attitude or the development of prejudice. Not to make decisions that cannot be made effective is to refrain from destroying authority. Not to make decisions that others should make is to preserve morale, to develop competence, to fix responsibility, and to preserve authority.[14]

There are, in short, too many calls on the president's time for functions which no one else at the college can perform for him to really be primarily "for the students." His major function must be to support his student personnel staff and his faculty so *they* can be "for the students," and then to get out of their way.

Of course, this is not to say that the president should turn his back on students. Their learning is what the college is all about and the more of them he can know personally, the better. If he can manage to do some limited

[14] Chester I. Barnard, *The Functions of the Executive* (Cambridge, Mass.: Harvard University Press, 1959).

teaching or lecturing, wonderful. His interest in students' lives and progress is important. But this is not something he can fake and the best president will not pretend to be something he is not. He is a fellow running a complex institution and he must continually ignite all its forces. He can be concerned for the student in trouble, but he must also be concerned for the staff member in trouble or the academic department in trouble or the college budget request in trouble. To pretend that he can give higher priority to the student in trouble than to the other troubles which come careening at him is to ignore the way an effective executive must function. The president must be "for the college" and the college must be "for the student."

Indeed, the relationship between the president and the students is less important than the relationship between the president and his faculty. He is first and last the head of a faculty. He should be the kind of person who attracts energetic, exciting teachers and with whom those teachers can flourish. The value of the president's teaching, if he can arrange to do some, may be greater because of its effect on his teaching colleagues than because of any magic in his personal instruction of students. I don't think his teaching constitutes unfair competition for his faculty colleagues as some presidents assert. If he can commit some of his time and energy to classroom teaching, he obviously feels it is more important than other things he might be doing. His commitment to the classroom inevitably will help to bridge the usual faculty-administration gap. It will let the students know, too, what the most important function of the institution is.

Many presidents say they just can't find the time to do any teaching, and in private residential institutions it may indeed be next door to impossible. But in a public commuting institution where fund raising and "hotel operating" responsibilities don't cause a drain on the president, some teaching may be feasible if the president wants to do it. Since we are avowedly teaching institutions, the community college president's participation in this primary function may be particularly apposite. The objection that the administrator will inevitably have to miss an occasional class because of unplanned for meetings or emergencies is, of course, a serious one. I have a solution for it, though, that seems to work pretty well for me. I *share* the teaching of a course in American Literature with a member of the full-time English faculty. Thus if I must miss he can pick up for me. The drain on me is cut in half, although I try hard to share fifty-fifty the "chores" of the course as well as the classroom teaching. I think the teaching of this course keeps me in focus as to what Berkshire Community College is all about as nothing else could.

There is a further advantage: a president who teaches reduces the danger of becoming a victim of the number one occupational hazard of college presidents: ennui. Henry Wriston describes in his book how he used to switch tasks periodically with his top associates at Brown in order to avoid becoming stuck in the mud of the annual cyclical routines of the job.[15] A fast-changing community college may not seem a place where boredom could be a problem. But for the mind, it may become one after half a dozen or so years. Teaching is an antidote to the ennui the same administrative job can come to have. It helps keep the intellectual light burning. (I'm reminded of the incomparable title of Dexter Keezer's book about his tour as president of Reed College: *The Light That*

[15] Wriston, *Academic Procession*, p. 156.

Flickers.[16] The first chapter should be required reading for all new college presidents; its title is: "How the Shirt Is Stuffed.")

If I were advising a community college board on selection of a new president, I would ask each one to put himself in the position of a perceptive, eager teacher with lots of choices as to where he could teach. Is this prospective president the man you'd choose to teach for? Never mind, for the moment, his knowledge of the nuts and bolts of education. Never mind the responsibleness or judiciousness his demeanor suggests. Will he attract a crack faculty? That's the first question, and incomparably the most important one. All other criteria for choosing the president should follow that one.

A final word: in one important respect the community college president must be unique: he must have or develop a real commitment to the value of two-year career or occupational programs. For he has a chance to lead his faculty and his somewhat inchoate institution into an area of service to society which will take on increasing importance as time goes on and as more and more high school graduates move on to post-secondary education. So far, the community colleges, including Berkshire, have talked much better than they have performed in career or occupational education. We have not really yet begun to educate sub-professionals and technicians in anything like the numbers needed. We'd better start soon, and I think we will. The trick will be for our community colleges to remain flexible enough and zestful enough and imaginative enough to meet the special new educational needs of the United States which community colleges appear

[16] Dexter M. Keezer, *The Light That Flickers* (New York: Harper and Row, 1947).

uniquely well-suited to handle. We must be in fact, as well as in name, "a new college for a new society."

For many of us in community colleges, the challenges we face are the most exciting in higher education.

Appendix A: Some Guides for Community College Campus Planning

California: "A Restudy of the Needs of California in Higher Education," California State Department of Education, Sacramento, 1955.

Colorado: "Guideline Procedures and Criteria for Campus Development and Capital Outlay Planning," prepared by the Association of State Institutions of Higher Education in Colorado in cooperation with Taylor, Lieberfeld and Heldman, Inc., New York, New York, April, 1964, mimeo.

Florida: Division of Community Junior Colleges, State Department of Education, "Suggestions for Preparation for a Building Survey in Florida's Community Junior Colleges," Tallahassee, February, 1963, mimeo.

Kansas: "Community Junior Colleges, A Report Relating to the Role, Function, Organization, Financing and Supervision of Junior Colleges," by the Advisory Committee on Junior Colleges to the Committee on Education, Kansas Legislative Council; Research Department, Kansas Legislative Council, Topeka, Kansas, October, 1964, mimeo.

New York: "Standards for Determining Space Areas,"

135

State University of New York, September 7, 1962, mimeo.

Rutgers Survey, "Guide for Planning Community College Facilities," 1964 (including a Checklist of 356 Questions), Division of Field Studies and Research, Graduate School of Education, Rutgers–The State University, New Brunswick, New Jersey.

Appendix B

Excerpts from A *Program of Educational Specifications*
Prepared for Berkshire Community College's New Campus
Presented to Architect Benjamin Thompson

This is a program of educational specifications (referred
to as our "Program") for Berkshire Community College's
new campus. It has been in preparation for a year and a
half by the college's New Campus Committee appointed
by the Chairman of the Berkshire Community College
Advisory Board.

The program is presented in the form of answers to
356 questions listed in the Rutgers "A Checklist for
Planning Community College Facilities." We regard the
Rutgers "Guide for Planning Community College Facilities" on which this checklist is based as a good starting
point for our planning and commend it to our architect.

Our BCC New Campus Committee was broken into
subcommittees and germane questions were assigned to
these subcommittees. Each subcommittee chairman prepared a statement of philosophy and purpose to introduce
his series of questions. A separate New Campus Committee Subcommittee, composed of the other subcommittee

chairmen, then reviewed these introductory statements and all basic questions in each category.

As an addendum to this program the BCC New Campus Committee is presenting to the architect a kind of "Basic Data Book" broken down into three categories:

1. Publications which are referred to in responses to specific questions in the list of 356 questions. For example, Educational Facilities Laboratories pamphlets giving specific description of something we'd like to see explored for BCC's new campus.

2. Publications and memoranda relating to Berkshire Community College: catalogue, brochures, faculty handbook, memoranda of college policy which we think the architect might wish to see, etc.

3. Publications describing the community the college serves: Pittsfield and Berkshire County.

While this program is being prepared in some detail, we would like to make it entirely clear that we regard it as merely a starting point for discussions with the architect. Our effort has been to address ourselves to key questions of college purpose and policy in order to reach tentative decisions as to just what it is we want in the way of a new plant. We wanted to avoid wasted time on the part of our architect in making us focus down on what we want. But the detail of this program should not be interpreted as rigidity on our part. We wanted to be specific but by no means binding.

What follow here are some general considerations:

1. THE STUDENTS

Our students are disparate: all ages, differing backgrounds, both sexes. There is a wide spread in their abilities and it will get wider as we offer less abstract career programs and attract to our new campus more very bright students. By and large, though, our students tend to be from the same socio-economic group and they are of course all from the same geographical area. They therefore tend to be parochial. Their college environment, like their faculty, should broaden their horizons.

2. THE FACULTY

Our faculty members double as student advisors. Much more of their time is spent, and should be spent, on sessions with individual students than in scholarly pursuits. The college should create a series of places including teaching facilities and faculty offices, where students can't help coming into easy and natural contact with faculty.

Our projected student-faculty ratio is sixteen to one. That ratio is a sound one for us. Let us use it for long-range plans. Fifteen-hundred students at sixteen to one equals ninety faculty positions. Note that many of the positions will be filled by several part-time faculty: Williams College faculty wives, for example.

3. THE COMMUNITY ASPECT OF OUR PROGRAM

Since a community college is the opposite of an "ivory tower," we should respond to the needs of our community. Specifically, we should fill those needs that are not now being met. Here are several particular plant needs of the community which the college can fill:

A. A *Little Theatre*. There is no really good little theatre with adequate stage and work areas in central Berkshire. There is, however, a vigorous little theatre group in Pittsfield, *The Town Players*, which is interested in cooperating with BCC on a theatre program.

B. *Art Gallery*. There is a felt community need for good art display areas, especially for contemporary work. The local museum devotes a good bit of its energy to an excellent natural history program. The college could serve as a "hub" for the creative arts in the Berkshires.

C. *A Field House.* There are excellent physical athletic facilities in central Berkshire. The local Boys' Club has recently built a new facility with a large basketball court, a good pool, an ice-skating rink. There are good YMCA, Catholic Youth Center, and Girls' Club facilities. But there is no large enclosed space for track, indoor softball, off-season tennis, etc. If such a space would double for large gatherings such as commencements, it would fill a real community as well as a college need. It should *not* be planned for theatrical or musical performances. (It might have a demountable wooden floor for basketball for the college, though this would probably not get much community use.)

Central Berkshire does need a large auditorium for musical performances. Presently a large auditorium at Pittsfield High School is used and for this purpose it is terrible.

Central Berkshire also needs a large banquet-type feeding facility. Our college center dining facilities will no doubt be called upon for community service, especially for groups on the campus for other purposes, e.g., conferences, etc.

4. The Evening and Summer Programs

The number of people taking courses in BCC's evening and summer programs will each be, as they are now, nearly as large as the daytime enrollment (1,500). So the atmosphere of the campus in the evening is terribly important. And year 'round plant use requires careful thought to temperature control during summertime. While we don't feel we can justify air conditioning in the Berkshires, except for some special areas (possibly the larger lecture halls), other means should be explored to keep us reasonably cool during July and August.

5. FUTURE EXPANSION

Places for 1,500 full-time day students will clearly serve our needs for a while, probably through 1975.

One approach to enrollment projection is to look at a formula for predicting enrollments which has worked for community colleges in the state of Washington and for Cape Cod Community College. The formula states that if one takes two-thirds of high school graduates for a given year within twenty-five miles of a community college, one has the total enrollment of the community college that year. Thus, using our local superintendents' projections, in 1968 BCC would have as its total enrollment two-thirds of 2,250, or 1,500. What conclusion to come to as to the future growth of the county and the concomitant growth of BCC? First, one can clearly predict that at some point, probably in the late seventies or early eighties, the college will have to expand. At some point, too, the college population will double. We have found it impossible to say when expansion and doubling will be necessary, though we have researched the matter carefully and have consulted with all local, county, state, and federal agencies who deal with population matters.

We feel after studying population trends that our architect should proceed on the assumption that the college will at some point in the next few decades expand in several stages to double its initial size of 1,500. The assumption should be that BCC will be *the* two-year college to serve the Berkshire County region and that it will not get large enough (say 5,000) to warrant the establishment of another community college in this region.

6. INSTRUCTIONAL AIDS AND MEDIA

We are prepared, after a great deal of discussion, to go pretty "far out" as to designing our teaching spaces to include the latest audio-visual aids and media. We have been impressed by what we have seen on other campuses and what we have been reading in the literature, particularly from the Educational Facilities Laboratories. The values of audio-visual aids have been shown and we want spaces that can best function to produce optimum educational results. This is particularly true for non-TV aids and media: projection devices (for motion pictures, film strips, and slides, and overhead, opaque, and shadow projections) and nonprojection devices (large scale models, demonstrations, apparatus, audio-recordings, radio, and teaching machines). We would plan to include science exhibits and mathematical models. So we would be amenable to exploring an audio-visual center. We want a good language laboratory and suggest that it might best be part of a facility for both in-class use like the Classroom and Studio Building at the University of Miami, Florida, *and* out-of-class study use, as the Benjamin Thompson–designed Phillips Andover Art and Communications Center is largely used. We go further and suggest that what we might need instead of such an audio-visual center and a library is one "Learning Resources Center" such as Florida colleges are developing.

7. "WE WANT" ITEMS

We list next a series of "We Want" items. This is a somewhat random listing of fundamental desiderata for the guidance of the architect: items which might not be specifically called for in any of the 356 questions.

We want to create natural rivalries among our students for extracurricular sports, one-act play contests, debates, etc. (How to do this? Semi-separate dining areas around a central kitchen?)

We want to use the beauty of our site to attract attention to ourselves.

We want to encourage community groups to use our campus for artistic and intellectual activities especially.

We want to create an evening atmosphere which will appeal to people, even without the spectacular views of the daytime hours.

We want a campus that is reasonably compact and efficient as a "teaching machine," yet we want to encourage outdoor use of the lovely site by students for walks, sports, socializing, etc.

We want as much flexibility as we can get in our teaching spaces, especially laboratories. (We like H. Peter Klein's analogy of spaces in a science building to the flight deck of an aircraft carrier.)

We want to respond to the critical need for post–high school career or occupational education, to encourage "noncollege material" students (an obsolete concept) to come to us for programs of a less demanding, less abstract, more practical nature than those we now have. See Norman Harris' book *Technical Education in the Junior College/New Programs for New Jobs*; we subscribe to the basic ideas it outlines. This emphasis on less abstract, more practical work means we must place particular stress on adequate shops and laboratories. See specific new occupational programs we plan to initiate under an "Introduction to Special Purpose Institutional Areas for Occupational Education."

We want BCC to be a center of learning in Berkshire County, so that whenever anyone here thinks of learning anything his thoughts will turn to BCC as the proper starting place.

—People concerned with conservation

—Builders wanting to find out about the latest materials

—People wanting to know more about foreign affairs

—Women wanting to learn how to cook better

—Engineers wanting up-dating course in their fields

—A young people's mineralogy club wanting to learn more

—Policemen preparing for civil service exams

—Teach-ins on whatever problems of our times

A sister institution we know of used to say that if you had twenty people who wanted any course at all, they'd put it on. That's what we want to do.

There is, however, one reservation. Where another organization is already doing a job well, we should not seek to compete with it or to duplicate its work.

There follow specific answers to questions in the Rutgers Checklist. (*Note:* Only a sample of the questions and answers are presented in this appendix.)

QUESTION 15

What essential outdoor areas must be considered in a community college campus?

—Parking

—Playfields of many sorts

—Paths for walking—all over site

—Areas for informal sitting, studying, socializing, sunbathing

—An outdoor amphitheatre

—An outdoor chapel or "contemplation place." There may be some good spots in the north portion of the site.

—Places where outdoor classes could be held by adventuresome teachers. Probably just lawn areas would

do, like our present Common. The outdoor amphitheatre might be used for this—or the chapel. This
is one of the purposes of the "exedras" of the University of Illinois Congress Circle campus in Chicago.
—Picnic areas
—Patios (used for outdoor dances at Harper College
in New York state)
—An outdoor eating area right outside the college center

QUESTION 18
Where should parking lots be located?
Around the periphery of the campus. The Foothill
Junior College (in California) arrangement seems excellent.
Obviously we don't want a "sea of cars." Good landscaping is essential. We must also consider snowplowing
problems in the Berkshires. (We plow our present lot
about eight to ten times per winter.)
We should have parking not too far from the theatre
and other buildings used extensively by the public.

QUESTION 22
Should there be special spaces for compact cars?
Yes. We will have to police our parking in some measure, we should think.
We also suggest special parking places, perhaps at the
corner of each parking lot, for bicycles and motor bikes.
We wonder about permitting bicycles and motor bikes to
be ridden on the campus. Our inclination is to forbid
both, but if we are spread out enough to warrant permitting them, perhaps special "bike paths" and bike racks at
buildings will be necessary.

QUESTION 23

How can the "mass effect" of many cars in the parking lot be made more aesthetically desirable?

Smaller peripheral lots as at Foothill Junior College, with planting (evergreens provide year-round screening). We could also move some earth around to screen out cars.

QUESTION 26

What building should be directly accessible to private cars?

None. The strongest argument can be made for the administration–guidance center and the theatre, but even there we don't think *direct* access is necessary. We'd say "reasonably close."

QUESTION 27

Should parking lots be illuminated at night? If so, to what degree?

Yes, Especially for evening classes it is important to have *good* illumination or women won't enroll. Safety and theft prevention dictate good lighting. We'd give this high priority.

QUESTION 29

Should vehicular roads, other than service roads, be allowed among the buildings?

No, for reasons of safety and expense of installation and maintenance.

QUESTION 31

Can service roads also double as student walks?

Yes.

QUESTION 36

Should certain trees be fenced off before construction begins to save them from destruction?

Yes! We hope we destroy *no* trees.

QUESTION 38

What are some of the main sources of noise that are disturbing to the instructional program?
—Cafeteria or lounge areas
—Student lockers (one reason for not having many student lockers)
—Utilities vents
—Other classrooms if walls not handled carefully
—Corridors unless they are handled carefully
—Student play areas
—Automobiles
—Poorly installed steam pipes

We'd give top priority to reducing noise problems for instructional areas.

We suggest using ceilings as sound-reflecting boards in classrooms for sound to bounce off, rather than placing acoustical tile on ceilings. Put acoustical material on walls and whenever possible use "acoustical flooring": carpeting.

QUESTION 46

Should academic departments be housed in separate buildings?

Not necessarily. Wherever feasible, *general purpose* classrooms should be used and faculty offices should be located together, not separated out so that art and chemistry people, for example, never talk.

QUESTION 47

Should there be certain zones for certain types of buildings (example: administrative zone, instructional zone, parking zone) to allow for added expansion or addition of certain types of facilities?

Yes, we feel this zoning concept must be followed to allow for expansion. While we see little need for immediate expansion, we will no doubt be expanding this campus sometime in the 1970's or early 1980's.

QUESTION 48

What plan (compact, cluster, finger, campus, etc.) is the most desirable for the physical plant of the college?

We will be guided by the architect on this one. We do like compactness, in general, and we like the cluster plan very preliminarily suggested by the architect.

QUESTION 49

What is the most desirable orientation of certain buildings to each other?

We tend to think BCC needs an inner-directed campus in order to encourage a feeling of community in these commuters. Amherst College has this sort of campus, but also has a fine external view—as we shall.

QUESTION 51

What are some of the dangers in the orientation of buildings?

Failure to obtain best view from other than classroom and laboratory buildings; excessive exposure to (a) sunlight in summer, or (b) northerly winds in winter; generation of problems for parking lots, access roads, and basic facilities, such as sewer and water. If buildings on the north portion are too far from West Street, excessive costs in roads and utility installation might result. On the other hand, if they are *not* up high, from some points on the campus one will look *down* on their roofs which may be undesirable from an aesthetic standpoint.

QUESTION 54
How should the insides of buildings be designed for flexibility?

Perhaps only exterior walls are load-bearing (or as close to this as is feasible).

Particularly in classrooms and laboratory buildings, basic services, such as water, electricity, telephone, gas, etc., should be available around the perimeter of the building with ducts under the floors to facilitate bringing this service to any part of the building where they are needed. Or these services might be carried in one central or peripheral duct complex, as in an aircraft carrier.

We like the idea of a field house rather than an auditorium and a gymnasium because of the flexibility that large enclosed general purpose space will provide.

QUESTION 61
Are enclosed walkways between buildings necessary?

Perhaps semi-protection would do, as at Benjamin Thompson's Bennington Regional School, or perhaps the idea of one complex in the form of a ⊔ would solve the problem better.

As a general matter, we are inclined to be against enclosed walkways. *Covered* walkways may be okay. They are used successfully at Henry Ford Community College at Dearborn, Michigan, where high winds prevail as they do at our site.

QUESTION 62

Are patios desirable between buildings? If so, what should be their function and what should they look like?

We think patios should be everywhere possible to encourage the mixing of faculty and students on an informal, spontaneous basis and to encourage people to "stick around" the college. We mean places with comfortable benches where people can sit to talk, smoke, read, eat lunch, study. The benches should have wooden seats (as opposed to stone or cement). Some should be in protected places—as on verandas made by the overhangs of buildings. Some should be in the open for catching the sun. In Mexico City in the middle of a large city park there is a Cervantes statue with benches with book niches in arms of the benches. The book niches presumably hold copies of *Don Quixote* but a similar design might be useful at some benches for holding "transients'" school books.

In outside areas there should also be lots of (unobtrusive) rubbish containers so that it is easy for people to get into the habit of throwing away lunch rubbish, waste paper, etc.

Attractive outside areas will be used for things never dreamed of. Did anyone in Benjamin Thompson's office plan for the Phillips Andover Art and Communications Center back yard to be used for football rallies, and the corner tree there for a grandstand, and the exterior stairs for a podium? That's one use it gets.

Outdoor places are sometimes especially attractive if they are above ground level—on a roof, for example. The sun decks at the Dartmouth Hopkins Center are popular.

Patios should flow easily from buildings. We've seen

some, especially in secondary schools, where you can't figure out how to get outside into them.

QUESTION 63

Should ramps or stairs be considered for the entrances into buildings?

Yes. We should make it easy for wheelchair students to come to us. This would mean one ramp into each building used by students. Once inside the buildings, service elevators could then be used.

QUESTION 67

What facilities should be available for use by community organizations?

All except administrative and maintenance areas. Thought must be given to having areas such as the theatre area discrete in the sense that community folks using the theatre cannot enter other unsupervised areas of the college buildings. Each such discrete area for community use must have adequate toilet and telephone facilities. This matter has been well worked out in two junior high schools in Pittsfield designed by Perkins and Will.

QUESTION 68

How much window area is desirable in buildings?

Lots of it in lounges, etc. Not so much in classrooms and other instructional facilities where it distracts. Perhaps in such areas it should only be along ceilings, so you get light and air without distractions. This is especially important if we are not to have air conditioning.

QUESTION 69

What "rule-of-thumb" figure should be used for determining lounge spaces?

We favor a multitude of relatively small, semi-discrete lounge spaces rather than very large lounge rooms. At the same time, lounge areas should be areas through which students naturally pass, rather than rooms into which one must consciously, and with a definite purpose, walk. They are, in short, semi-corridors, semi-discrete rooms. Each space should be large enough for easy chairs for several people. Chairs should be deep and comfortable so as to give a real change of mood from the school seats. Outside of the library, cafeteria, and such places, there should be *ten to fifteen lounge chairs per hundred students*. This would eliminate the concentrations of noise and congestion that render college lounges usually so much like smoking cars on poor trains.

QUESTION 70

In what buildings should lounges be provided?

Principally in the college center. But "lounges" in the sense of small, pleasant areas for sitting while waiting for a faculty member near his office, or even for a class to start in a classroom fairly distant from the student center, are desirable. The Education Building at the University of Illinois has very pleasant waiting areas at the end of each corridor of this (essentially faculty office) facility. They were in constant use when we saw them. In contrast, we saw many students sitting on the corridor floors of classroom buildings at the University of Illinois Chicago campus while waiting for classes to change. Lounges were too far away.

The Physical Education area may be far enough away from other facilities to warrant some lounge space.

In *any* lounge area, there should be good light for studying or reading.

QUESTION 76

Is a public address system essential to a community college?

No.

QUESTION 77

Should there be a bell system for the entire campus?

A *carillon*, perhaps as part of a water tower? (*Not* a bell system in the traditional school sense.)

We have literature on carillons for discussion with the architect.

Perhaps the carillon–water tower could become the symbol of the college. It might have a clock on it and its bells would call people to class, etc.

QUESTION 79

What areas should have clocks?

One clock at each end of a hall on all floors in instructional areas; several in the student center including at least one in the cafeteria; principal general offices; field house; principal maintenance building; laboratories and library.

We do *not* want clocks in classrooms, lecture halls, theatre, nor in individual administrators' or faculty members' offices.

QUESTION 81

Should building exteriors be illuminated at night?

It might be nice to floodlight the carillon tower and/or one or two key campus buildings at night, especially if this would support the illumination program for preventing vandalism and making people, especially women, "feel" safe.

QUESTION 82

What areas on the campus should be fenced?

None until a playing field is used for events to which admission is charged. Don't fence parking lots; snow removal is then difficult. Should we have an outdoor swimming pool, it must be fenced.

QUESTION 87

Can corridors be used for other purposes?

1. Note under "college center" that we suggest lounge areas be semi-corridors. That is, areas students *pass through* normally, *not* discrete rooms into which one must go.

2. Corridors in classroom buildings might be put on outside wall rather than between two classroom strips. Temperature, light, etc. then easier to control in the classroom.

3. They can be used for strips of bulletin boards to insure some privacy for offices adjacent to glass corridors, as at University of Illinois Education Building.

4. Display areas for exhibits, bulletin boards. If wide enough, they can even be small instructional areas, but we have doubts about this because of distractions. Delta College does this but we don't think it would work for us.

5. Stephens College uses corridor walls in its learning center for art displays. Walls are lined with plywood-backed fabric.

6. Possible fall-out shelter area.

7. Pegs or open-type racks for clothes.

QUESTION 90

Should there be provisions for small and large group instruction?

Yes. We are for classrooms of all possible useful shapes and sizes. We think it diminishes the monotony of spending many hours of each day in class. Also we think that different types of seating should be designed in.

The learning experience in a seventy-five-seat lecture hall is different from that in a twenty-five-seat classroom. Both kinds of learning are important.

We do feel, though, that community college freshmen and sophomores are less ready to be "on their lonely own" in a large lecture situation than upper-division students (or Harvard College lower-division students). We are therefore being somewhat conservative in our classroom size choices. Much more conservative than we would be if we were building a program for a selective four-year college or university.

There should be variety in size so that each class can be scheduled in the size room that offers (1) no compromise in quality of instruction and (2) greatest economy in use of faculty time. Because some basic BCC classes (e.g., English composition, foreign languages, and speech) are best taught in small groups (20–25) there will be need for *twelve rooms designed for a maximum of twenty-five students*. (Much intimacy and give and take are lost when twenty students are scheduled in a room large enough to accommodate, say, fifty.)

There will be need for *twelve rooms designed to accommodate a maximum of forty students*. These rooms will be used for those classes which, for a variety of reasons, should not be taught in large lecture sections and yet do not require that the enrollment be as low as twenty or so.

We feel that once a class size has exceeded forty it might just as well be built up to seventy or beyond if it can be scheduled in a carefully designed room that will utilize a high percentage of the seating space. (This is to eliminate the displeasing experience of speaking to partially filled rooms.) For this reason we want *three lecture halls of seventy-five seats, one of 150 seats, and one of 250 seats.* (Any group exceeding 250 will be scheduled in the little theatre which will seat 500, and which will be scheduled mornings only, 8:00 A.M.–noon, for lectures in order to be free for rehearsal use at other times.)

QUESTION 91

Should small general purpose instructional rooms with a maximum capacity of fifteen students be programmed?

We want three small seminar rooms adjacent to offices of department heads for faculty departmental meetings which would then double as small seminar classes for students. An office of the Law Dean at the University of Illinois is used in just this flexible way.

QUESTION 92

What subjects can be taught in these areas?

A large variety of subjects, particularly where enrollment happens to be low. We won't purposely *schedule* many low-enrollment classes, but some inevitably turn up each semester. They can use these seminar-conference rooms.

QUESTION 97

Should the type of student seating purchased make a difference in the size of instructional spaces?

1. We favor sloped floors for seventy-five-seat lecture

halls and above. We understand that above 100 seats, sloped floors are pretty much essential.

We also favor "wrap-around" seating for everything above forty-seat classrooms. Note, too, under "special purpose instructional facilities" that some of the forty-seat classrooms are to be used as science lecture-demonstration halls. These may have to have sloped floors or "wrap-around" arrangements, also.

2. As a general matter, we like tablet armchairs. They are flexible, comfortable, you can't slouch, they can be pushed close together for "rapport." There are tablet armchairs which have fixed legs which are quite economical of space.

3. The three small-capacity classrooms to be furnished with overstuffed chairs for relaxed discussions will necessarily be larger than a room designed for the same number of tablet armchairs.

4. We do like variety in seating. It makes otherwise similar classrooms seem different. Architect Walter Netsch has done this very well at the University of Illinois Chicago Circle campus. We also like the use of the multi-shaped tables which can be rearranged as the faculty member wishes.

QUESTION 100

Where should general purpose instructional areas be located?

1. Any place in the academic area. These rooms should be for use of all disciplines requiring them.

2. Where located next to corridors, leave no glass doors that tend to create distractions each time a person walks by or stops to look into the room.

QUESTION 108

What provisions should there be (in general purpose classrooms) for audio-visual aids?

We want a good bit of emphasis on audio-visual aids. Projectors for slides, movies, opaque, shadow, overhead, and film strips. Overhead projectors are particularly useful located *in* the classroom if the instructor is to use the aid on his own, "manually," during the class. IBM classrooms at Endicott, New York, have one in every room. Thus they are used. It must be made as easy as possible for a faculty member to plan, get at, and use the aids.

A tiny ceiling spot at each student writing station can provide illumination when the room is darkened. Or table arrangements with lights at each student station.

QUESTION 109

What special color treatment is recommended for these areas?

Avoid pastel blue—too cold. Warm colors are better—yellow, cream. *Variety* is important. The colors in our present building do lend variety. They are a bit bright but "pick up" our old building. That won't be as necessary in the new classrooms. Students, brightly dressed, tend to "bring their own colors with them," as architect Hugh Stubbins says.

QUESTION 115

What provisions for flexibility in instructional areas should be considered?

1. Changes are from semester to semester, or more likely year to year, rather than hour to hour or day to day. We suggest cinder-block walls (non-load-bearing) between two twenty-five-seat classrooms. We could, say, fairly easily take out the wall and have one sixty-seat class-

room (one teaching station less). Put a row of tile on the floor and a row on the ceiling and we are in business.

2. Colorado College provides flexibility through its four-foot-wide wall to carry utilities in its Olin Science Lecture Hall. For science and technical offerings this would give us needed flexibility for the long pull.

QUESTION 117

What type of regular classroom facilities or laboratories requires library corners for ready reference?

1. Especially important for science rooms and labs, art and design, music and drama.

2. Perhaps open storage for books as well as other items would suffice. Particularly since we don't want any suggestion of splintered library facilities and services. We don't want departmental libraries. We want *one central* library.

3. Why not an unabridged dictionary and stand in each teaching room?

QUESTION 118

What subjects will be taught in these (physical education) areas?

Physical education at BCC will be required of all students for at least two semesters. Emphasis in the program should be placed on general physical fitness and the teaching of techniques and skills of carry-over sports such as golf, tennis, badminton, volleyball, skating, skiing, fencing, etc.

Intramural athletics should stem from the physical education program. Individual and team competition will be promoted and organized on the basis of the needs and desires of the students with the emphasis on broad participation in large numbers.

Intercollegiate athletic teams will be an outgrowth of the intramural program and will probably never be more than moderately extensive. Varsity teams in basketball, baseball, and possibly lacrosse, soccer, track and cross-country are the most likely. Individual sports such as tennis, golf, fencing, skiing, etc., will be developed as student interest develops. No great demand for spectator seating is foreseen and football is never likely to be a varsity sport for many reasons.

The program will require an indoor facility, preferably a large field house, of sufficient size and flexibility to accommodate both men and women in large numbers in a variety of activities. In the fall this would provide a large dirt floor for rainy days, as well as a number of utility rooms for indoor activities. In the winter a portable board floor occupying about half the dirt floor would provide an area for basketball and leave room for other activities. In the spring, the dirt floor would provide indoor baseball facilities, indoor tennis, and areas for other sports in inclement weather. A swimming pool is desirable and would be very useful if not too expensive.

The field house should be adaptable for large gatherings such as commencements and convocations. It might have an organ and perhaps a way of flying flags which "pick up" an otherwise uninteresting area. Edward Stone has used flags effectively in his dorms at the new State University campus in Albany. (It might also be used for "laboratory" aspects of the Building Construction Occupational Education Program. See Introductory Statement on Special Purpose Instructional Facilities for Occupational Education.)

Outdoor playing fields should consist of a baseball field, a quarter-mile track, and several spacious general playing areas. There should be at least six hard-surface tennis courts and an area reserved for a golf-driving range and/or four or five rudimentary practice fairways and greens. One area, with some elevation, should be reserved for a modest ski run with perhaps a rudimentary lift. Cross-country skiing will be a natural. Provision should be made for storage of skis.

Of interest is the cost, utility, and practicability of "inflated bubbles" for use as covers for tennis courts, swimming pool, and other facilities. The performance and cost of upkeep would definitely be factors of importance as would their appearance.

Addendum to "Physical Education and Athletics"

We noticed that some of the parking lots at the University of Buffalo had basketball backboards along the periphery. Although those parking lots were used pretty heavily for student parking during the times we observed them, it seemed to us that the backboards were probably put there for use when the parking is not quite so heavy. This strikes us as a good idea and the expense of putting up a backboard on an already blacktopped area would obviously not be too heavy. Our guess is if it were pretty carefully thought through as to which areas would get heaviest parking and which would get lightest, it might be worthwhile to put up some basketball backboards along the periphery of the blacktopped parking areas on our new site where parking would be called for only during heaviest student hours, for example.

QUESTION 187

What are the purposes to be served by the Student Center?

BCC as a commuter college needs facilities for student activities that give students maximum opportunity for "campus life" and the contacts normally provided by dormitories and living centers at campus colleges. As a nucleus for this, we suggest a central building designated as the *College* Center rather than the *Student* Center. It should be close to the Administrative-Guidance Center, the closer the better.

The College Center should provide a favorable climate for faculty-student contacts in meeting rooms, lounges, the cafeteria, the bookstore, and the game rooms. With this in mind, five meeting rooms and three offices should be available, not only for student government and student publications, but also for departmental clubs and interest groups. These eight spaces should be flexibly arranged to respond to changing student needs for organizational headquarters or for community or college meeting places. One of these areas might be used as an alumni office. While there should be a faculty dining area, service would be provided through the same cafeteria line as for students. Ample provision should be made for Cokes, coffee, and snacks at all hours in attractive areas conducive to serious conversation and small talk.

The bookstore should be part of the College Center and it should be large and attractive. It should carry, in addition to texts and essentials, a large collection of paperbacks covering all areas of learning and culture.

One concept for the principal lounge in the College Center could be to develop it as a showplace—the focal center of the building. The "Top of the Hop" in the Hopkins Center at Dartmouth College is an excellent lounge in this sense. In keeping with its setting in the Berkshires, it might well center around a large fireplace. Further, its location might well be such that a panoramic outlook through picture windows would result. It should be open to student traffic, not a "cave."

A game room or recreation room providing space for

dancing and equipped with table tennis, card tables, pool table, and TV should be adjacent to the main lounge, possibly with sliding partitions to provide one large facility when required, though we are in general somewhat leery of sliding partitions.

Adjacent to the main lounge should be located a small utility kitchen or pantry equipped with heating units, cupboards, sink, table, etc., so that coffee and tea and light refreshments can be easily prepared for social affairs in the lounge without needing access to the regular cafeteria or kitchen. The utility kitchen could also serve our new General Bartlett Room, a formal social-meeting room like the room in our present facility. This should be adequate for social gatherings of fifty people, or for meetings for twenty-five.

Appropriate spaces should be provided for a trophy case, bulletin boards, and a central control desk for reception.

QUESTION 194

Should the student cafeteria be in one large room?

No. We would favor several smaller rooms for the student cafeteria. One large room tends to be architecturally uninteresting, not at all cozy or "fun to be in." Smaller rooms are more quiet, more interesting, and more easily able to cope with luncheon meetings, etc.

Probably there is no activity that will go on in the whole college that will be better able to take advantage of nice views than eating. Let's have some really nice views from our eating places.

Let us also try to have a sidewalk cafe or roof terrace or veranda for eating outside.

Our idea of fostering natural rivalries among our student

body might be fostered by separate semi-discrete eating areas.

The New Commons Building designed by Hugh Stubbins at the University of Massachusetts seems to us to create semi-discrete areas successfully by planning the kitchen centrally and putting dining areas all around it. One big area *seems* like smaller areas.

QUESTION 197

What types of provisions for serving meals should be considered (lunches, snacks, banquets, full-course dinners, etc.)?

All types of service should be considered, but we are primarily a luncheon-serving institution. At one time or another the college dining areas will be used for all. Banquets for really large groups are probably not our function.

As long as food is kept hot and service is fast, we don't favor any particular system. Can the plates themselves be kept hot?

Someone once said three ingredients make a dinner party: hot plates, a cold room, and low flowers.

QUESTION 199

Should there be separate faculty dining rooms in the center?

Yes, *semi*-private, for thirty seats. This in addition to a private conference-luncheon room for twenty, for faculty committee meetings, etc. The *semi*-private area might be set off by glass partitions. The assumption is that some faculty will eat there, others will "spill over" into regular student eating areas.

QUESTION 203

How long should food service facilities be available to accommodate the evening program students?

As long as any building is in use. Vending machines are probably best for this 'round-the-clock coverage.

QUESTION 204

What types of display areas should be located in the student center?

Display areas in the college center should include one closed official bulletin board, and a large open space for student posters and notices. Also, provision where practicable for displays of paintings, photographs, etc.

For a good model of display areas well set up, the Hopkins Center at Dartmouth College is suggested.

QUESTION 206

How should lounge furniture be placed?

Lounge furniture should be placed with emphasis on informality and comfort. Small groupings around a fireplace and in front of picture windows. If there are patio-type areas near lounges, special outdoor furniture must be available or students will move indoor furniture outdoors and we'll all be sorry.

QUESTION 219

Where on the campus should the administrative facilities be located for the most efficient service?

As centrally located as possible for use by faculty and students. Visitors may have a short but pleasant walk. The parking area for visitors need not be right next to administration facilities, but the walk should not be long. These facilities should be close to student mailboxes for easy communication. Find a reason to keep students moving through this building, not just for special notices which frighten them.

Administrative offices need not be lavish. If economies must be effected, here is a good place, rather than in areas that serve students more directly. While they must be good *working* spaces, with good light, ventilation, and acoustical treatment, they need not be the kind of "prestige" space which many colleges feel they must have. The president's office, for example, need not be the lush, cavernous, impressive place it is in many colleges.

Easy movement from one office to another is important. So is flexibility; administrative space needs change rapidly in a college, perhaps even more rapidly than career teaching space needs. While we have been fairly specific and detailed in the answers that follow, we do hope we can get flexibility to make changes in office arrangements as the organizational arrangements of the college shift in the future.

Nor should the administrative spaces be so isolated that there is a feeling of "inner sanctum" about them. Students should be made to feel comfortable approaching them. We propose tying them to the guidance offices. It is a natural tie for a community college whose primary function, after teaching, is guidance. A prejudice will be seen in the answers that follow against counters between students and administrative people they deal with. We treat the students in an open, friendly manner, as adults. As a result they behave as adults. We want our new campus to reflect this relationship.

QUESTION 233

What are some other factors that should be considered in planning the administrative area?

Some of the student personnel offices should open directly on a corridor so students may come directly in when doors are open.

If possible, there should be an arrangement by which a student coming out of the Dean of Students' office could do so without going through the main waiting area. The point is that it is nobody's business that a student comes in for an interview if he is troubled.

QUESTION 234

Where should the guidance facilities be located for maximum efficiency?

At a central point on the campus in the flow of student traffic, preferably in the same complex with administrative offices.

Our emphasis is on bringing administrative and guidance functions together and on having the guidance offices be the hub for guidance work which goes on primarily in faculty offices. Our real guidance people are our faculty. The Dean of Students and his aides are those to whom faculty refer students whose problems seem beyond the regular advisor. Academic *advising* (as contrasted with personal *counseling*) will be done almost entirely by faculty. Along with teaching, that is their function. But they will inevitably do a good bit of personal *counseling* as well, though there they will often need help from the Dean of Students and his associates.

That is why we want to bring the guidance headquarters together with those of the Dean of Faculty and his division heads in Liberal Arts, Business, and Engineering and Technology, and why we want the faculty lounge close by. In our college the faculty have as much to do with the Dean of Students on guidance matters as they do with the Dean of Faculty on teaching matters. So the

Dean of Students' complex must be a place where *faculty* come and go constantly. Like students, a faculty must be made to feel "at home" there. On a given day, a faculty member might come into this administrative-guidance complex to see *both* the Dean of Faculty and the Dean of Students, or their aides. It should be easy and natural for him to do both with one trip from his own office.

QUESTION 245
What provision should there be for faculty offices?
1. Every full-time faculty member should have a private office. We'd give this *top priority*.
2. The point should be kept in mind that these offices are primarily for private counseling with students. Acoustical treatment is therefore very important. They should be readily accessible to students. They should not all be put together in a complex of offices which has a forbidding, unapproachable feeling.

QUESTION 246
What should be the size of the faculty offices?
More important than *size* is *arrangement*. Ninety square feet can seem plenty spacious and can be very efficient. We suggest all faculty offices be ringed with brackets so all kinds of things can be hung up. Bookcases, shelves, pictures, even desks in the form of pine boards can be fixed to them. All kinds of different working arrangements can be made. Perhaps if we plan carefully, typical offices of ninety square feet will do. If it is desired to have the faculty usually on the premises—and it is—then attractive offices are essential. Last, the nature of the college teacher's work is such that he tends to acquire paraphernalia; his office is necessary for its convenient storage.
Each office should have a mail slot in the door for

regular mail and intracollege communications which will be handled by students.

QUESTION 248

Do all faculty members need similar space?

All offices should be the same *size*. Six department chairmen will have adjacent conference or seminar rooms.

Some faculty appear to prefer relatively "monastic" offices: no windows to distract. We might have some offices like this, some with views.

QUESTION 256

Should separate department libraries be established? If so, where and what size?

If so, they should be in the main library. Shelves in classrooms for books and other materials in classrooms and seminar rooms should cover the need for *separate* material. We want the campus *compact* enough to have the central library the location for departmental collections.

QUESTION 257

Should there be office space for part-time evening instructional staff?

Yes, shared desks with part-time day faculty. These areas should have coat racks and pleasant informal chair arrangements for sessions with students.

QUESTION 263

What types and sizes of storage space are necessary for the custodial and maintenance staff?

Serious consideration should be given to the possibility of installing suction tubes to all areas of the buildings. Such a system eliminates the necessity of having in each area of the building large mechanical vacuum cleaners.

With a suction tubing system custodians merely carry the wand section of a vacuum with a long flexible hose to the area to be cleaned and merely attach the hose to the suction coupling in the wall. Such a system is not only quicker and less tedious for a custodian, but it also eliminates the need for a large number of mechanical vacuum cleaners as well as the storage area necessary for them.

QUESTION 265

How extensive should be the health services that are offered?

We cannot and should not provide much service in the way of student health facilities. The beauty of a commuting college is that it can be stripped down to educational essentials and therefore can cost less money to build, less to run, and less to attend than a residential college. The assumption is that the student lives at home, or, if not, that he is on his own for sleeping, for looking after himself as to personal behavior, and for taking care of his own health needs. The dollars the college gets from the state for his education, plus the few he contributes himself, must be spent on the activities that go on in the classrooms and laboratories and on the extracurricular activities which extend the learning he does in classes and labs. The myriad ancillary services provided for the residential students are not offered the commuting student.

Obviously, one can carry this stripped-down philosophy too far. We do offer meals and encourage social activities, and some of our psychological counseling is pretty extensive and "expensive." And there is a kind of paradox here in that while we are stressing our cold-hearted attitude toward providing certain kinds of services to our students, our success so far has largely been built on the intimate, friendly atmosphere which students find at BCC. But if we are to use our limited budget wisely and take advantage of our unique opportunity to concentrate on educational essentials, our posture must be that we *cannot* have a psychiatrist on our staff to provide help in depth to troubled students; that we *cannot* get involved in an elaborate, expensive intercollegiate athletic program; and that we *cannot* offer any more than the most rudimentary kind of health service.

QUESTION 282
What types of services and materials should be available in the community college library?

1. A soundproofed room for typing for students to use.

2. Several display cases—for new books, etc. These cases should be both in the library and in its approaches.

3. A "Docustat" twenty-five-cent, thirty-second reproducer of material.

4. Tapes, records, films. For records, listening booths or tables with earphones should be considered.

5. Microfilm readers.

6. Adequate tables and carrels.

7. A special room for teaching machines and aids for programmed learning.

QUESTION 283
Where should the library be located?

Somewhere in the heart of the campus where people can move to it easily. *Not* so that people must use it as a thoroughfare. Not split in any way by a corridor.

QUESTION 290
How should the number of volumes in a library be determined?

The American Library Association recommends 20,000 volumes per 1,000 students excluding duplicates; 5,000 volumes for each additional 500 students. We'll plan to have room for 40,000 volumes.

QUESTION 356
What should be the educational environment for a comprehensive community college?

Benign.